Dear Mental Health Professional:

This protocol is part of the *Best Practices*™ series that is designed to provide mental health practitioners with empirically based treatment programs. We have edited this series to be clear and user friendly, yet comprehensive and step-by-step.

The series offers high quality, consistently formatted protocols that include everything you need to initiate and complete treatment. Each session is outlined in detail with its own agenda, client education materials, and skill-building interventions. Each session also provides sample instructions and therapist-client dialogues.

The therapist protocol you are using corresponds with an available client manual that is designed to be used concurrently. Your protocol has all the worksheets, homework assignments, in-session treatment exercises, and didactic material that is in the client manual. Also included are pre- and post assessments, and an overall program evaluation. An appendix contains a treatment plan summary (now required by many managed care companies).

Ten *Best Practices*™ protocols are currently available or in development. They include protocols for PTSD, GAD, OCD, agoraphobia/panic disorder, specific phobia, social phobia, depression, anger management, BPD, and eating disorders.

We wish you every success in using this program with your clients.

Sincerely,

Matthew McKay, Ph.D.
John Preston, Psy.D.
Carole Honeychurch, M.A.

OVERCOMING
SPECIFIC
PHOBIA

■

A Hierarchy and
Exposure-Based Protocol
for the Treatment
of All Specific Phobias

Edmund J. Bourne, Ph.D.

Distributed in the U.S.A. by Publisher's Group West; in Canada by Raincoast Books; in Great Britain by Airlift Book Company, Ltd.; in South Africa by Real Books, Ltd.; in Australia by Boobook; and in New Zealand by Tandem Press.

Copyright © 1998 by Edmund J. Bourne, Ph.D.
New Harbinger Publications, Inc.
5674 Shattuck Avenue
Oakland, CA 94609

Cover design by Poulson/Gluck Design.
Edited by Carole Honeychurch.
Text design by Michele Waters.

ISBN 1-57224-114-4 Paperback

New Harbinger Publications' Website address: www.newharbinger.com

First Printing

Grateful thanks to Matt McKay for conceiving and organizing this project; and to Carole Honeychurch for a thorough and skillful job in editing the manuscript.

Finally I am indebted to my partner, Jane, for her support, encouragement, and for carefully processing several drafts of the text.

Contents

Introduction

Overview of the Disorder

Major Clinical Features

Specific phobia involves a strong fear and avoidance of *one particular* type of object or situation. Most often, the phobic situation is avoided, though in some instances it may be endured with dread. Confronting the object or situation almost always provokes anxiety.

With specific phobia, fear is generally focused on the *phobic situation* itself and only secondarily, if at all, on having a panic attack. This is unlike agoraphobia, where the primary focus of fear tends to be on panic attacks. There is also no fear of humiliation or embarrassment in social situations, as in social phobia. Panic attacks may occur with specific phobia, but only upon confronting the feared object or situation.

While fears are pervasive, a diagnosis of specific phobia is made only when the fear and avoidance are strong enough to interfere with normal routines, work, relationships, and/or cause significant distress. Complete diagnostic criteria for specific phobia are indicated in *DSM-IV* (1994) as follows:

Diagnostic criteria for 300.29 Specific Phobia

A. Marked and persistent fear that is excessive or unreasonable, cued by the presence or anticipation of a specific object or situation (e.g., flying, heights, animals, receiving an injection, seeing blood).

B. Exposure to the phobic stimulus almost invariably provokes an immediate anxiety response, which may take the form of a situationally bound or situationally predisposed Panic Attack. Note: In children, the anxiety may be expressed by crying, tantrums, freezing, or clinging.

C. The person recognizes that the fear is excessive or unreasonable. Note: In children, this feature may be absent.

D. The phobic situation(s) is avoided or else is endured with intense anxiety or distress.

E. The avoidance, anxious anticipation, or distress in the feared situation(s) interferes significantly with the person's normal routine, occupational (or academic) functioning, or social activities or relationships, or there is marked distress about having the phobia.

F. In individuals under age 18 years, the duration is at least 6 months.

G. The anxiety, Panic Attacks, or phobic avoidance associated with the specific object or situation are not better accounted for by another mental disorder, such as Obsessive-Compulsive Disorder (e.g., fear of dirt in someone with an obsession about contamination), Post Traumatic Stress Disorder (e.g., avoidance of stimuli associated with a severe stressor), Separation Anxiety Disorder (e.g., avoidance of school), Social Phobia (e.g., avoidance of social situations because of fear of embarrassment), Panic Disorder With Agoraphobia, or Agoraphobia Without History of Panic Disorder.

Specify type:

Animal Type

Natural Environment Type (e.g., heights, storms, water)

Blood-Injection-Injury Type

Situational Type (e.g., airplanes, elevators, enclosed places)

Other Type (e.g., phobic avoidance of situations that may lead to choking, vomiting, or contracting an illness; in children, avoidance of loud sounds or costumed characters)

Subtypes

Specific phobias are classified into five different types:

Animal Type: This category of phobias consists of fears of animals such as snakes, mice, or dogs, or insects, such as bees or spiders. Typically, animal phobias originate in childhood.

Natural Environment Type: These phobias consist of fears related to the natural environment, such as heights (sometimes referred to as acrophobia), fire or water; or natural occurrences such as thunderstorms, tornadoes, or earthquakes.

Blood-Injection-Injury Type: In this category are fears evoked by the sight of blood or seeing someone injured. Phobias of receiving an injection or other invasive medical procedures are also included. These phobias are grouped together because they are all characterized by the possibility of fainting, in addition to panic or anxiety. Blood-injection-injury phobias can develop at any age.

Situational Type: Situational phobias relate to a variety of situations in which a fear of being enclosed, trapped, and/or unable to exit plays a dominant role. Such situations include flying, elevators, driving, public transportation, tunnels, bridges, and other enclosed places such as shopping malls. Situational phobias tend to develop in childhood or in early adulthood (twenties).

Other Type: This is a residual category for specific phobias not falling into the previous four types. Included here are fears of contracting illness (such as AIDS or cancer), avoidance of situations that might lead to choking or vomiting (for example, eating solid foods), and the fear of open spaces.

In clinical settings, these five subtypes are not equally prevalent. Among adults, situational and natural environment types are by far the most commonly seen, with an occasional client presenting with a blood-injury or animal phobia. Among children, natural environment and animal phobias are common.

Etiology

There are at least four types of predisposing causes of specific phobias. A common origin is *trauma*, as in the case when fear of flying develops after a traumatic experience with flying, or fear of driving follows being in a car accident. Merely witnessing a traumatic event *(observational learning)* may also be sufficient to lead to the development of a specific phobia. For example, seeing the devastation of an earthquake or witnessing the remains of a plane crash on television has been known to engender specific phobias in some persons. *Modeling* can also be a cause. Repeated observation of a parent with a specific phobia can lead a child to develop that same fear.

Still another common cause is *classical conditioning.* Having a spontaneous panic attack while traveling through a tunnel or being caught in an undertow while swimming, for example, can result in phobias of these situations. Anxiety-provoking encounters with dogs, snakes, bees, spiders, thunderstorms, loud noises, darkness, or costumed characters may cause specific phobias in children.

Most specific phobias can be traced to three types of themes:

1. Fear of injury, harm, or death

2. Fear of being trapped and/or losing control because you are trapped

3. Fears of something strange or unusual, outside the expected range of ordinary experience

Fears related to abandonment, humiliation, or rejection appear less common with specific phobia. Such themes are primarily associated with agoraphobia and social phobia.

Prevalence and Gender Ratio

The prevalence of phobias in the general population is approximately 9 percent. The lifetime expectancy of experiencing a phobia is about 10 to 11 percent. In a majority of these cases, the phobia does not interfere with the individual's life or does not cause sufficient distress to meet the diagnostic criteria for specific phobia.

Gender ratios vary across subtypes of specific phobia. For situational, natural environment, and animal phobias, approximately 75 to 90 percent of cases seen are female. One exception is fear of heights, where 55 to 70 percent of cases are female. Also, approximately 55 to 70 percent of individuals with blood-injury-injection type phobias are female. Data for prevalence of specific phobias across subtypes is unavailable as of this writing.

Treatment Approach

A general treatment approach that has been used successfully to help people overcome phobias, and the theoretical model used here, is commonly referred to as *cognitive behavioral therapy* (CBT). The "cognitive" part of CBT developed in the early eighties out of efforts to extend Aaron Beck's cognitive therapy of depression (Beck, 1979) to the treatment of panic attacks and generalized anxiety (Beck and Emery, 1981). Cognitive therapy focuses on correcting misappraisals of body sensations perceived as threatening and on teaching clients to identify, challenge, and counter erroneous cognitions that aggravate anxiety and worry. The "behavioral" aspect of CBT consists of techniques designed to reduce physiological anxiety such as breathing retraining and relaxation training, along with the desensitization strategies described below: systematic desensitization and *in vivo* exposure.

Systematic desensitization was developed by Joseph Wolpe, a South African psychiatrist, in 1958. Wolpe assisted anxious people to develop a hierarchy of stressful scenes related to their phobia. The hierarchy ranged from scenes that produced almost no anxiety to images that were strongly anxiety-provoking. After training clients in progressive muscle relaxation, Wolpe helped them to desensitize to the scenes one by one, by pairing them with deep relaxation. Systematic desensitization was the dominant method for treating phobias during the 1960s and early 1970s. It is still used today as a preparation for *in vivo* exposure or in instances where it is difficult to implement real-life exposure (e.g., phobias of earthquakes or tornadoes).

Exposure therapy (also called contextual therapy) was developed during the 1970s out of the pioneering work of Art Hardy on the west coast and Robert DuPont at the National Institute of Mental Health in Maryland. Like systematic desensitization, exposure relies on a graded hierarchy of situations ranging from mild to intense in their potential to evoke anxiety. Unlike Wolpe's method, exposure involves repeated confrontation with, or approach to, the phobic situation in "real life." Frequently the therapist or a support person accompanies the client during the early stages of exposure, and then gradually withdraws to assure the client obtains mastery over the situation on their own. Exposure therapy has consistently outperformed systematic desensitization as a treatment for both agoraphobia as well as specific phobias (Barlow, 1988) to the point that it is currently the dominant approach for treating phobias of all kinds.

Cognitive behavioral therapy is foremost an *educational* approach to treatment. It involves teaching clients two things: 1) *concepts* that can help them to better understand and cope with their difficulties involving anxiety, and 2) *specific skills* that enable them to confront and master problems with panic attacks or phobias. Skill mastery requires compliance on the client's part in carrying out weekly homework assignments.

For purposes of this protocol, only cognitive behavioral therapy is considered as a treatment approach because of its excellent track record with specific phobias. Other treatment approaches, including hypnosis and eye-movement desensitization have been used to treat phobias with some success. The interested reader can consult books by Hadley, Lucas, and Shapiro (see references) for detailed discussions of these approaches.

Medication is often used in conjunction with cognitive behavioral therapy to treat anxiety disorders, especially in the case of panic disorder, agoraphobia, and obsessive-compulsive disorder. However, medication is not a major strategy in the treatment of specific phobias; its application will be briefly described in a later section.

Treatment Components

Diaphragmatic Breathing

Clients are taught diaphragmatic breathing as a technique to contain physiological symptoms of anxiety both in advance of and while confronting their phobic situation. Two skills are taught: 1) learning to breathe from the abdomen, and 2) using a count on the inhale and exhale to ensure breathing is slow, regular, and unforced. There is a controversy as to whether the anxiolytic effects of breathing retraining lie primarily in the realm of direct symptom reduction versus increasing the client's sense of control. In an extensive review of breathing retraining, Garssen, de Ruiter, and van Dyck (1992) concluded that controlled, diaphragmatic breathing worked primarily by providing distraction and increasing perceived sense of control.

Progressive Muscle Relaxation

In addition to diaphragmatic breathing, clients are routinely taught progressive muscle relaxation (PMR), a shortened form of Edmund Jacobson's original technique involving progressive tensing and relaxing of sixteen different muscle groups (Jacobson, 1974). The primary application of PMR in the treatment of specific phobia is its use in systematic desensitization. In order for desensitization to occur, the client couples anxiety-provoking scenes with deep relaxation. Thus, imagery desensitization is always preceded by ten to fifteen minutes of PMR.

It has been found that an alternative form of PMR known as *passive muscle relaxation* is as effective as the traditional form where clients actively tense and release various muscle groups. In the passive form, clients receive direct suggestions (live or taped) to relax specific muscle groups, usually starting with the feet and working up to the head. More detailed instructions for both active and passive forms of progressive muscle relaxation can be found under session 2 of this treatment program.

Anxiety Coping Skills

Because situational panic attacks are always a possibility with specific phobias, clients are given instruction in panic-management strategies. (In communicating with the client, it is preferable to speak of "anxiety coping skills" rather than "panic management.") Part of this training is conceptual. The idea is stressed that a panic attack is caused by a misattribution of danger to the physiological symptoms of anxiety. If the client is able to endure unpleasant symptoms of anxiety, such as rapid heartbeat, constricted breathing, sweaty palms, dizziness, and so on, without labeling such sensations as dangerous—or potentially catastrophic—it is possible to minimize the likelihood of a panic attack. Much emphasis is given to the idea of *accepting* rather than struggling against or trying to avoid symptoms of anxiety. The more it is possible to accept what happens when symptoms begin to arise, the easier it is to "ride them out."

The second aspect of panic management involves skill mastery. Clients are encouraged to practice abdominal breathing and/or positive coping statements such as "I can handle these symptoms," in response to mounting anxiety. It is important for clients to understand that these skills require considerable practice in low-anxiety situations before they will become effective in the context of high anxiety or panic. Clients are also encouraged to use conventional distraction techniques such as: 1) talking to their support person, 2) moving about, 3) observing what's going on in the immediate environment (to reinforce staying in the present), and 4) getting angry at symptoms, to divert attention away from anxiety-provoking thoughts and sensations. While there is some evidence that exposure is slightly more effective without distraction from internal thoughts and sensations (Craske et al. 1989), my experience indicates that distraction techniques can be very effective in enabling clients to undertake and persist with the exposure necessary to master many types of specific phobias (especially fear of flying). Distraction techniques seem to be particularly helpful in the *early* stages of exposure. Toward the end of exposure training, when clients have already achieved some degree of desensitization, they can be encouraged to focus on residual symptoms of anxiety. By not distracting themselves from such symptoms (which is still a subtle form of avoidance), further desensitization may be attained.

Systematic (Imagery) Desensitization

Systematic desensitization is a behavioral method for treating phobias first developed by Joseph Wolpe in the late 1950s. It combines relaxation with a structured process of gradually confronting a phobic object or situation, most often through imagery. The client is asked to visualize an incremental series of scenes relating to the phobic situation, which vary in intensity. For example, in the case of a phobia of injections, the client might start off visualizing a doctor's office, followed by a scene of someone else getting a shot, and concluding with a scene of receiving a shot themselves. Actually, there are usually eight to twenty scenes which increase very gradually in their fear-evoking intensity. This is what Wolpe first referred to as a *stimulus hierarchy* (later shortened to just *hierarchy*). By visualizing the scenes in a relaxed state, the client is able to unlearn conditioned anxiety responses to the phobic situation (desensitization) and relearn a more relaxed mode of response.

There is considerable research support for systematic desensitization in the treatment of phobias. After successful completion of an imagery hierarchy, clients usually overcome their phobic avoidance without future regression. In some cases, their systematic desensitization employs direct rather than imaginal exposure to a phobic object, especially in the case of animal phobias of dogs, snakes, or insects.

In the 1970s the use of direct, real-life exposure, structured through a hierarchy of incremental steps, came to be called exposure therapy. Today exposure is the dominant mode of treatment for phobias, although systematic desensitization is used in cases where direct exposure is impractical or impossible (for example, phobias of natural disasters).

In Vivo *Exposure*

Real-life exposure is the most powerful and effective intervention for overcoming specific phobias. While all of the components described here are needed for optimal treatment effectiveness, exposure therapy is the heart and soul of successful treatment. Exposure involves establishing a hierarchy of progressively more demanding confrontations with the client's phobic object or situation in real life. The client then works up through the various situational exposures, usually accompanied by a support person. For example, in dealing with a fear of flying, the hierarchy might begin with looking at pictures or movies of airplanes or perhaps going to the airport. It would end with taking a real flight of one or two hours' duration. In between would be a graded series of exposures including, for example, visualizing all the elements of a flight or boarding a grounded plane.

Exposure has been conducted in various ways. Two possible variations include: 1) massed vs. spaced practice sessions, and 2) controlled escape vs. sustained (non-escape) exposure.

Massed vs. spaced exposure

It is possible to conduct exposure in an intensive format, having the client enter into the phobic situation for one or two hours every day for seven to ten days. More common is a weekly format: doing therapist-assisted exposure once per week with homework assignments for the client to practice exposure (with or without a support person) several times between therapy sessions.

Research investigating massed vs. spaced exposure has been mixed. Foa, Jameson, Turner, and Payne (1980) found superior effectiveness for massed exposure, at least on a short-term basis. On the other hand, Barlow (1988) suggested that spaced exposure is preferable because dropout rates are lower and the likelihood of relapse following treatment is somewhat less. Chambless (1989) conducted a comparison study and found essentially no difference between the two formats.

Controlled-escape vs. sustained exposure

Controlled-escape exposure involves allowing the client to retreat temporarily from the phobic situation if anxiety reaches a critical threshold, then return to the situation after anxiety diminishes. This method of exposure is employed in the TER-RAP program for treating agoraphobia (1986); it was developed by one of the founders of exposure therapy for phobias, Art Hardy. It is also the method used by this author and recommended in this protocol. Sustained exposure (also called "endurance" exposure) involves encouraging (not forcing) the client to remain in the phobic situation no matter how intense his or her anxiety level. The idea is to endure anxiety (even if it becomes panic) until it subsides. The client presumably learns that they can survive any degree of anxiety, which helps them to reduce their perception of danger regarding anxiety symptoms. This form of exposure has been employed by many therapists beginning with Robert DuPont's contextual therapy in the late 1970s. A good statement of the endurance approach can be found in Jerilyn Ross' popular book *Triumph Over Fear* (1994). In my experience, a problem with the endurance style of exposure is that it can lead to resensitization to the phobic situation if a client has a full-blown panic attack during exposure. It also can discourage some clients from further practice. Those who prefer the endurance approach maintain that this is rarely a problem.

Research does not come down strongly on either side of this issue. Emmelkamp (1982) found subjects did best if they were instructed to terminate exposure when anxiety reached "unduly high" levels. However, Rachman, Craske, Talman, and Solyom (1986) obtained equally effective results whether subjects retreated from exposure when anxiety reached 70 on a 0–100 point scale (provided they returned to the situation following retreat) or if they were instructed to stay in the situation until anxiety peaked and then diminished by 50 percent. Still, the subjects in the controlled-escape group had greater perceived control and less fear during exposure (as might be expected) than the endurance group. To the extent that perceived control and self-efficacy are the "curative agents" in the cognitive behavioral approach to treating phobias, then a strategy that maximizes perceived control and minimizes fearful arousal might be preferred. Craske and Barlow (1993) conclude that "exposure can proceed effectively without eliciting and then habituating relatively high levels of fearful arousal." In my experience, exposure is significantly easier to conduct if clients are allowed to temporarily retreat from prepanic and panic levels of anxiety.

Exposure therapy has both an educational as well as a practice component. First, the client, with the therapist's assistance, develops a graded hierarchy of exposures respective to their specific phobia. As with systematic desensitization, the hierarchy has eight to twenty steps, beginning with a very minimal approach to the situation and ending with an exposure likely to elicit high levels of anxiety (e.g., for fear of flying, making a two-hour flight; for acrophobia, riding an elevator to the top of a skyscraper; for blood-injection phobia, having several vials of blood drawn). Next, the client is given explicit instructions on how to conduct exposure, using the controlled-escape approach described above. In addition, the client is taught a series of guidelines presenting basic concepts and attitudes that are helpful to anyone undertaking exposure. These guidelines are presented in detail in treatment session 6. Finally, the client's motivation and any resistance toward exposure are explored.

Wherever possible, the therapist accompanies the client while the client undertakes exposure, using the therapy hour each week to complete one or more exposures in the established hierarchy. When logistics prohibit the therapist from assisting the client, it is incumbent on the therapist to train a relative or friend of the client to be a support person. Even if the therapist does conduct exposure in session, such a person is needed to assist the client with exposure practice between formal therapy sessions. Usually the prospective support person comes with the client to a session and receives training from the therapist on how to function as a support person during exposure. There are, to be sure, some instances when the client can complete their exposure hierarchy on their own. However, the therapist needs to be prepared to support most clients during the early phases of exposure, either in person or by training someone else to do so. (Some larger treatment centers have paraprofessionals trained to accompany clients during exposure.) Detailed guidelines for educating support persons are presented in session 7.

Cognitive Restructuring of the Content of the Phobia

Desensitization and exposure are the primary strategies for undoing conditioned fear reactions and avoidance associated with a phobia. However, cognitive restructuring of the specific beliefs around phobic avoidance can often assist clients in gaining confidence to undertake and maintain exposure practice. Clients are first taught the concept that every unreasonable fear has two components: 1) *overestimating* the odds of a negative outcome upon facing the fear, and 2) *underestimating* one's ability to cope when confronting the feared object or situation. At least one session of therapy (usually prior to undertaking desensitization) is devoted to identifying, challenging, and countering both types of distorted cognitions. A list of constructive counterstatements is drawn up which the client rehearses at home during the week. These counterstatements may subsequently be used both during and in anticipation of exposure.

To illustrate, suppose that a client is fearful of flying, both because of a fear of the plane crashing as well as feeling confined while on board the aircraft. Statistics on the odds of dying in a plane crash (approximately 1 in 7 million) are presented to challenge the client's perceived risk of flying. Then, the client's belief of being confined is reframed as follows: The feeling of being "trapped" is often due to an excess of energy (due to a high state of physiological arousal associated with anxiety) which needs expression in a situation where movement is difficult (driving a car in stop-and-go traffic or standing at line in a grocery store are similar examples). By expressing this energy—i.e., *going with* rather than resisting the autonomic mobilization response associated with panic, the sense of being trapped can actually be diminished. Thus, even though it is not possible to get off the plane, it *is* possible to reduce the perception of being trapped by getting up frequently to walk up and down the aisle during the flight (provided, of course, there is not excessive turbulence).

In addition to reducing the perception of entrapment, the client and therapist review and practice a number of strategies that are likely to increase the client's belief in his or her ability to cope with anxiety during a flight: abdominal breathing, the presence of a support person, and distraction techniques such as magazines, puzzles, or a cassette player with a relaxation tape.

In sum, by giving attention to restructuring the beliefs and perceptions which maintain a specific phobia, the task of exposure is made easier.

Worry (Anticipatory Anxiety) Coping Skills

The most reliable way to overcome anticipatory anxiety associated with a phobia is to master the phobia itself. It is useful to instruct clients that their anticipatory anxiety around facing what they fear will go away once they've completed their hierarchy and fully desensitized to the situation. Prior to full desensitization, it is important to teach clients coping skills they can use to reduce worry during the weeks or months it takes to work through their hierarchy. Briefly, these techniques include: 1) thought stopping, 2) deferment of worry, and 3) distraction techniques such as physical exercise, conversation, or any other activity that can divert and absorb one's attention. These techniques are discussed further in session 4.

Research

Systematic desensitization was developed by Joseph Wolpe in the 1950s. It is a "mastery" model, the goal of which is to completely eliminate anxiety in the target situation. Early research showed that 80 percent of subjects who underwent systematic desensitization were "cured," with another 10 percent "improved." (Agras 1985)

The focus on mastering anxiety is simultaneously the strength and weakness of systematic desensitization. Patients feel a sense of accomplishment and freedom when they are able to face formerly frightening situations with little or no anxiety. On the other hand, they have no skills to cope with anxiety if it reemerges or is encountered under different circumstances.

An alternative, and equally effective, form of systematic desensitization was developed by Donald Meichenbaum (1974). He called it *stress inoculation*, and it was based on a "coping" model of anxiety management. Instead of shutting off images of phobic scenes at the first sign of anxiety (as in systematic desensitization), Meichenbaum taught patients to stay in the stressful scene. They learned to cope with and diminish anxiety through relaxation and cognitive restructuring. Stress inoculation has the advantage that the patient's new coping skills can be applied to any anxiety-evoking situation.

We now know that systematic desensitization, or any similar imagery-based treatment, is usually not sufficient to cure phobia. These treatments are only effective in so far as they motivate patients to expose themselves to the feared situation (Agras 1985). They are often helpful in a role of preparing the client to face the more difficult *in vivo* exposures. But they are always adjunctive techniques.

In vivo exposure is the central ingredient in the treatment of phobias, and it is more effective than any alternative procedure (Emmelkamp 1982; Mathews et al. 1981; Mavissakalian and Barlow 1981). Follow-up studies show that treatment effects are maintained over periods of more than four years (Emmelkamp and Kuipers 1979; Jansson and Ost 1982; Munby and Johnston 1980; Jansson, Jerremalm and Ost 1986).

Duration of Treatment

Clinical experience as well as research support a minimum treatment program of ten weekly sessions. This is the minimum time necessary for the client to master all of the concepts and skills relevant to undertaking *in vivo* exposure, as well as completing at least a few weeks of exposure practice itself. The protocol described here includes ten sessions (with the option of one follow-up session) as follows:

1. Intake Interview (Initial Assessment)
2. Breathing and Relaxation Training
3. Cognitive Restructuring of Phobia Content
4. Anxiety/Worry Management Skills
5. Imagery Desensitization
6. *In Vivo* Desensitization (Exposure)—Education and Set Up
7. *In Vivo* Practice (includes training support person in session)
8. *In Vivo* Practice
9. *In Vivo* Practice
10. Review and Closure

In many cases, completion of exposure may require more than ten sessions; the purpose of this protocol is to provide a *minimal framework* for effective treatment.

Note: Some therapists may opt to omit imagery desensitization and begin exposure a week sooner. This allows more time to complete exposure by the the end of ten weeks. It is my preference, in most cases, to include imagery desensitization because it often helps clients to more easily undertake exposure.

When the constraints imposed by the client's financial resources or managed care do not allow for ten sessions, the protocol can be abbreviated to a six-week format as follows:

1. Intake and Breathing Retraining
2. Relaxation Training and Anxiety/Worry Management Skills
3. Restructuring Phobia Content *or* Imagery Desensitization
4. *In Vivo* Desensitization (Exposure)—Education and Set Up
5. Train Support Person with Client in Session

6. Follow-up and Troubleshoot Initial Exposure Practice
   (leave option for one month follow-up)

This very abbreviated program requires good time management on the part of the therapist in order to telescope what is usually done in three sessions down to the first two sessions. In session 3, a choice needs to be made between imagery desensitization or restructuring phobia content, depending on which intervention the therapist deems most useful to the client. In fear of flying, for example, restructuring the client's beliefs about the risk of air travel might take priority. However, with a fear of snakes, imagery desensitization may be necessary before the client is willing or confident to attempt confronting toy or real snakes. Since this abbreviated format does not allow time for the therapist to conduct *in vivo* exposure, the success of treatment depends on training a significant other or friend of the client to fulfill that function (session 5). The final session reviews and "troubleshoots" the initial *in vivo* practice session with the support person. Then the client is given the option of reporting back at a later time (usually one month) to follow up on the effectiveness of ongoing exposure practice.

Assessment

The first consideration in evaluating any client presenting with a phobia is correct diagnosis. Is the problem truly a specific phobia or is it a manifestation of panic disorder with agoraphobia? This differentiation can be difficult because both disorders can include panic attacks and avoidance of similar types of situations. Five criteria can be used to make the distinction:

1. *Onset:* Panic disorder with agoraphobia typically begins with unexpected or spontaneous panic attacks. Avoidance develops secondarily out of a fear of confronting certain situations perceived as likely to cause panic attacks. Specific phobia, on the other hand, begins with avoidance of a particular situation. Panic attacks do not occur spontaneously but only in the context of confronting the feared situation. For example, if a client comes to your office complaining of panic attacks when he rides the elevator to his job on the eighteenth floor, a brief history can establish the correct diagnosis. If panic attacks occur only in the context of the elevator, a diagnosis of specific phobia is likely. If the client has experienced spontaneous panic attacks or panics in situations other than elevators (with some degree of avoidance of such situations), the diagnosis would be panic disorder with agoraphobia.

2. *Focus of Fear:* In panic disorder with agoraphobia, the focus of fear is typically on having a panic attack across several different types of situations. In specific phobia, the focus of fear tends to be on the particular dreaded object or situation, although there may be a secondary fear of having a panic attack or losing control in the situation.

3. *Type and Frequency of Panic Attacks:* Panic disorder with agoraphobia tends to be characterized by spontaneous panic attacks that occur weekly or

daily. In specific phobia, panic attacks are situational, occurring only when confronting the avoided situation.

4. *Number of Situations Avoided:* Panic disorder with agoraphobia typically involves avoidance of more than one situation (e.g., driving far from home, grocery shopping, being home alone). A specific phobia is, by definition, an avoidance of *one* particular object or situation, although clients may present with two or three separate specific phobias (e.g., a fear of snakes, flying, and water).

5. *Presence of Generalized, Continuous Anxiety:* Persons with panic disorder—with or without agoraphobia—are often anxious and hypervigilant much of the time between episodes of panic. Persons with specific phobia tend to be anxious only when confronting the phobic object or situation.

Sometimes there may be a concern in differentiating specific phobia from social phobia. In social phobia, the focus of fear is invariably on a fear of negative evaluation. Specific phobias, on the other hand, generally do not involve fears of negative social appraisal. Thus, if a client presents with a fear of eating in restaurants, it's important to evaluate the focus of fear. If the concern is with being embarrassed or negatively evaluated by others, the diagnosis is social phobia. If the fear is focused on choking, it is a case of specific phobia (other type).

If a child is fearful of being separated from significant others, the appropriate diagnosis is separation anxiety disorder, not specific phobia.

If a person is fearful of contracting a disease such as AIDS or cancer, the correct diagnosis is specific phobia (other type). On the other hand, if the person has the conviction that they already have a disease, the appropriate diagnosis is hypochondria.

Finally, it is important to keep in mind that specific phobia is diagnosed only when the phobia causes significant impairment in work or social relationships—or when it causes significant emotional distress.

It is important to evaluate the client for other co-morbid psychiatric conditions such as dysthymia or substance abuse disorders. Even if the client requests treatment for specific phobia, these other disorders (especially substance abuse) take precedence in treatment. Such problems need to be resolved before addressing the specific phobia.

Beyond diagnosis, there are six areas that need to be evaluated at the time of the first session in order to develop a satisfactory treatment plan. A more detailed structured interview covering these areas is presented later in the description of the initial session.

1. *History of the Phobia:* This includes the date of onset and circumstances which led to initial development of the phobia. It also includes the progression of the phobia from onset up to the present time, with emphasis on any circumstances that aggravated or decreased phobic avoidance. Any co-existing medical conditions should be noted, particularly if they are likely to have an impact on the client's ability to do exposure (i.e., disabilities that limit mobility).

2. *Current Level of Impairment:* an evaluation of the client's current degree of avoidance. For example, does the client avoid elevators altogether, travel only to the second floor, or do they endure riding elevators, but with high levels of anxiety? How does avoidance vary with the presence or absence of a support person accompanying the client? Does the client experience panic attacks when confronting their phobia? What is the client's level of anticipatory anxiety in advance of confronting the situation?

3. *Prior Treatment:* a history of previous attempts to obtain professional help and their outcome.

4. *Prior Coping Strategies:* a description of coping strategies that the client has devised to try to handle their phobia on any occasions when it was necessary to confront it.

5. *Use of Medication:* includes any medications the client has used to assist in facing their phobic situation. Was medication used continuously or on an acute basis only? At what dose?

6. *Current Resources:* includes the client's motivation, any secondary gains that could strengthen resistance to treatment, client locus of control (do they take responsibility for overcoming their problem or expect the therapist to "fix" it?), support of immediate family (do family members understand the phobia and support the client's recovery?), and availability of a support person (does the client have a family member or friend that can accompany them during the initial phase of *in vivo* exposure practice between therapy sessions?).

Patient Self-Rating Scale

The first session is the ideal time to gauge the severity of the client's symptoms. The questions that make up the initial assessment are very important, but a more precise measurement may be obtained using the following questionnaire.

The following evaluation instrument allows you to calculate a numeric rating of the client's emotional reaction to their phobia. The instrument was adapted from the Fear Questionnaire (Marks and Mathews 1978). In a sample of twenty phobic patients Marks and Mathews report a mean score of 5.5 for the global phobic rating (question 7) and 22 for anxiety and depression (questions 1 through 6). A subsequent study of twenty-six phobic patients found an average reduction of 2.6 points for the global phobia rating and a reduction of 6 points for anxiety and depression, following treatment.

Have the client choose a number quantifying the intensity of each of the six feelings listed. Then the client makes a global severity of symptoms rating (question 7). This requires an understanding of what phobic symptoms are, which you should have covered before administering the questionnaire. The questionnaire should be completed now, at appropriate intervals during therapy, and in the final session of therapy. This data can be very affirming for both the client and the therapist, and may prove valuable in demonstrating the protocol's efficacy to managed care institutions.

Fear Questionnaire

In regard to your phobia, choose a number from the scale below to show how much you are troubled by each problem listed, and write the number in the blank.

0	1	2	3	4	5	6	7	8
Hardly at all		Slightly troublesome		Definitely troublesome		Markedly troublesome		Very severely troublesome

_____ 1. Feeling miserable or depressed

_____ 2. Feeling irritable or angry

_____ 3. Feeling tense or panicky

_____ 4. Upsetting thoughts coming into your mind

_____ 5. Feeling you or your surroundings are strange or unreal

_____ 6. Other feelings (describe)

7. How would you rate the present state of your phobic symptoms on the scale below? Please circle one number between 0 and 8.

0	1	2	3	4	5	6	7	8
No phobias present		Slightly disturbing/ not really disturbing		Definitely disturbing/ disabling		Markedly disturbing/ disabling		Very severely disturbing/ disabling

Adapted from the "Fear Questionnaire" by I. M. Marks and A. M. Matthews, 1978.

Specific Goals of Treatment and Limitations

It is important to establish explicit treatment goals by the end of the first session. These goals are always specified by the client; the therapist's stated role is to assist the client in achieving his or her goals for therapy. In the case of specific phobia, the goal is usually straightforward and easy to define—i.e., overcoming avoidance of the specific feared object or situation. There are, however, two levels of goal attainment possible: coping or mastery. Coping means the ability to confront and handle the phobic situation with some degree of anxiety. Mastery means the ability to negotiate the phobic situation with little or no anxiety. Mastery is obviously a higher level of "coping" and is easier to achieve with some phobias—and with some clients—than others. *In general, mastery is only attainable when frequent exposure to the phobic situation is feasible.* This is not always possible. Frequent exposure may be limited by logistic and financial constraints, as in the case of fear of flying. Or it may be limited by natural constraints, as in the case of a fear of tornadoes or earthquakes. It is critical to let the client know that complete, 100 percent recovery from a phobia may be unrealistic if it is not possible to conduct a sufficient number and frequency of exposures to ensure complete desensitization. In short, the expectation for a full recovery from a fear of heights or elevators is usually higher than it is for a fear of some type of natural disaster or taking a professional exam. It is nearly always possible to cope with a phobia, that is, to stop avoiding the situation. Mastery—the ability to handle a phobic situation with little or no anxiety—is another matter.

The protocol described here applies only to specific phobia. Yet, in real life, it's more an exception that the *primary* goal of treatment is simply to overcome one specific phobia. Many clients with anxiety disorders present with multiple issues, including two or more coexisting anxiety disorders and/or depression. If a client presents with a fear of flying, injections, or contracting an illness in the context of agoraphobia, then treating panic disorder and agoraphobia takes precedence. Differential diagnosis of specific phobia from agoraphobia is one of the first orders of business during the initial session. Treatment for specific phobia should also be *secondary* to treatment of other anxiety disorders—i.e., panic disorder without agoraphobia, social phobia, obsessive-compulsive disorder, or post-traumatic stress disorder, since all of these disorders require considerations and interventions that do not apply to specific phobia (for example, panic disorder and obsessive-compulsive disorder usually require both cognitive behavioral and pharmacological interventions not relevant to specific phobia). Treatment of depression also should take precedence over addressing specific phobias since depression typically impedes a client's ability to complete and follow through with the rigors of exposure therapy. Finally, if a client presents with substance abuse, marital problems, or an adjustment disorder *and* specific phobia, it is advisable to respond to the other problem first unless the client expressly wants treatment only for the phobia. (In the case of substance abuse or significant interpersonal issues, I generally refuse to offer treatment for a specific phobia until the more pervasive problem is cleared up.) In short, overcoming a specific phobia is the *primary* goal of therapy only in those cases where all other diagnoses have been ruled out. When a client presents with more than one diagnosis, the order and precedence of treatment goals should be clarified at the outset.

In some cases, a client, having no other diagnosis, will seek treatment for two or more separate specific phobias (e.g., fear of snakes, fear of flying, *and* a fear of blood or injections). In these cases it is important to identify what the client's priorities are, that is, which phobia is most important for them to address first. In my experience, it is preferable to work on only one phobia at a time, though time and/or financial constraints may dictate otherwise.

Three kinds of limitations can arise in the treatment of specific phobias. First, it may be difficult to achieve real-life exposure because the feared object or situation occurs infrequently—for example, fear of natural disasters, fear of thunderstorms, or fear of a professional licensing or certification exam. In such cases it is necessary for the therapist to use some ingenuity in devising *simulations* of real life through imagery, audio, or video tapes of the feared situation. For example, I once treated a client phobic of lightning with audio and video tapes of thunderstorms. (We were clear at the outset that complete desensitization might not be possible unless he chose to live in an area where thunderstorms were frequent for a period of at least a few months.)

A high-tech alternative is to use the recently developed technique of *virtual exposure.* Virtual exposure uses a computer-based technology devised to generate three-dimensional simulations of the phobic situation. This approach has been used by Barbara Rothbaum at Emory University to treat acrophobia (fear of heights). Three settings were simulated in virtual reality: 1) a glass-walled elevator at a high-rise hotel, 2) balconies with railings from the ground up to the twentieth floor, and 3) footbridges over a river. Over eight weekly therapy sessions, clients spent as much time as they needed in each virtual situation for their anxiety to diminish. They were found to have physiological reactions and subjective experiences quite similar to those that occur during *in vivo* exposure. Experimental clients showed significantly greater desensitization than controls on all measures following treatment. The potential advantage of virtual exposure is convenience for the client and easy simulation of almost any type of phobia. However, the technology is presently much too expensive (approximately $100,000 for the prototype system) to be available to most therapists. Personal computers appeared about twenty years after mainframe prototypes; perhaps in a few years the use of virtual exposure will be common.

A second common limitation is the unavailability of a support person to accompany the client during *in vivo* exposure practice sessions. In some cases treatment may have to be postponed until such a person can be found. I have encouraged clients, when family and friends were unavailable, to seek out a support person (who could subsequently be trained) by contacting volunteer service agencies or advertising at local colleges or in the newspaper. It is important to let clients know at the outset that they will need someone to assist with exposure, apart from the therapist, in order to complete assigned practice sessions. While unassisted exposure is sometimes possible, it is not something either the therapist or client should count on, especially when avoidance has been long-standing and anxiety about exposure is high.

Finally, treatment may be limited by financial constraints. The client may not be able to afford the minimum of ten to twelve sessions necessary for effective treatment. The sample treatment plan at the end of this therapist manual (appendix 4) may help in getting the requisite number of sessions approved by managed care providers. Failing this, see the abbreviated treatment format described in the previous section on duration of treatment.

Agenda Setting

Establishing an agenda at the outset of the session is important. It creates a context for the focused, highly structured approach required by cognitive behavioral therapy. Each session begins with a clear agreement between therapist and client on what is going to be accomplished during the hour. In a brief therapy protocol, it is incumbent on the therapist to be directive and focus on specific tasks to be completed for the session (for example, training in relaxation or imagery desensitization). With clients who are prone to tell personal stories, this may require continuous refocusing back on the task for the session. Clear agenda-setting early in the session is essential to establish the expectation that the session is about concept and skill mastery rather than a recounting of the past week's events or other stories. Of course, this kind of structured approach has its limits. Any significant crisis in the client's personal life will take precedence. Feelings need to be expressed and worked through to the point where the client is able to set aside life concerns and refocus on cognitive behavioral concepts and skills. It is always important to take into consideration the client's current emotional state and his or her present life concerns, so that therapy is not perceived as overly rigid or insensitive. Balancing the need to stay on task with being empathetic and sensitive to the client's feelings and concerns often is one of the more challenging aspects of doing effective time-limited therapy.

Homework

Critical to the success of brief, structured therapy is the client's completion of assigned homework. In the treatment of specific phobias, behavioral homework assignments are given at the end of each session. For example, the client is asked to practice abdominal breathing skills, cognitive restructuring of the erroneous beliefs maintaining their phobia, or the first step or two of their exposure hierarchy. Completion of assigned homework is reviewed at the outset of the following session. Problems encountered in doing homework are discussed and resolved (see "Review of Homework" sections under treatment sessions 2–10 below). By reviewing homework at the *beginning* of each session, the client is given the message that completion of homework is a critical part of the therapy.

It is important *not* to judge the client according to whether they complete homework assignments. The therapist always give the client responsibility for utilizing therapy. It is the therapist's role to keep reiterating that if homework is not done, the client is unlikely to derive much benefit out of therapy. If the client wants to utilize therapy sessions only for supportive listening and venting of feelings, rather than overcoming their phobia, that is their choice. However, it is important that both therapist and client are clear about what the nature of the therapy is—effective treatment of a phobia is only possible if homework assignments are completed.

When clients do their homework, it is important to acknowledge and validate them for doing so. When they don't, it is vital to explore their resistance—what is getting in the way. Understanding the client's resistance may lead to some of the richest insights about underlying attitudes and mind-sets that may be affecting the client's self-esteem, relationships, and general success in life. In some cases, these issues need to be addressed and resolved before the client can seriously undertake structured, cognitive behavioral therapy. When such issues are present, the expectation of completing phobia treatment in ten sessions is unrealistic.

Compliance with homework may also be improved by giving the client a self-monitoring form that they bring to each session. On the form they can check off those days between sessions that they completed the practice of a particular skill. This enables both client and therapist to acknowledge the client's investment and commitment to doing assigned homework during the week. A sample form appears on page 20.

Concurrent Pharmacological Treatment

Of all the anxiety disorders, specific phobia least often requires adjunctive use of medication. Specific phobias tend to be acquired as a result of trauma or classical conditioning and usually do not involve the kind of chronic neurobiological imbalance that can contribute to other anxiety disorders such as panic disorder, agoraphobia, generalized social phobia, obsessive-compulsive disorder, or post-traumatic stress disorder.

As a general rule, it is useful to proceed with treatment without reliance on medication. The primary exception to this is when the client encounters considerable difficulty undertaking or sustaining *in vivo* exposure. When anxiety reaches *panic* levels every time the client attempts exposure, it may be useful to use a low dose of a high-potency benzodiazepine such as Xanax or Ativan. A low dose usually means .25–.5 mg. Higher doses than this may suppress all sensations of anxiety to the point that desensitization cannot occur (it is necessary to experience some anxiety in order to desensitize).

Medication is used only to mitigate anxiety in the context of exposure—i.e., the client takes the medication fifteen to twenty minutes prior to beginning the exposure session and not otherwise. Since clients with specific phobia rarely experience high levels of anxiety apart from confronting their phobic situation, there is generally no need for ongoing use of anxiolytic medications between exposure practice sessions.

The temporary reduction of anxiety achieved by using the medication just prior to exposure may be sufficient to enable an otherwise resistant client to get started.

When high-potency benzodiazepines are used, two things are important to emphasize. First, medication is only a temporary aid to the early stages of exposure. Full mastery of a phobia requires the ability to face the situation without medication. After the client has worked through his or her hierarchy with medication, it

Weekly Practice Record

Goals for Week   Date:

1.

2.

3.

	Mon.	Tues.	Wed.	Thurs.	Fri.	Sat.	Sun.
Practiced abdominal breathing technique (6–7 times)							
Practiced deep relaxation technique (6–7 times)							
Used anxiety management strategies*							
Practiced worry management techniques*							
Countered negative self-talk (used "Worry Worksheet")*							
Practiced imagery desensitization (3–5 times)							
Practiced exposure (3–5 times)							

*Recommended frequency varies depending on focus

will be necessary to rework all the steps without the use of medication if the client wants to attain full mastery of the situation. (In phobias that involve infrequent exposure, such as flying, some clients may opt for medication every time they face the situation. This is a "coping"—not a "mastery"—outcome, and sometimes it is all the client wants.)

Second, it is important that the client not view medication as a substitute for learning anxiety-management skills that are necessary to handle anxiety during exposure. Without such skills, the client will likely relapse when exposure is attempted without medication. Many clients develop greater confidence in their ability to handle their phobia if they achieve full mastery—the ability to comfortably negotiate a situation that was once avoided—without the use of any medication. Again, for clients who are satisfied to simply cope, situational use of medication may be a useful strategy.

In general, tricyclic and SSRI antidepressant medications, which are often useful in the treatment of panic disorder, agoraphobia, generalized social phobia, obsessive-compulsive disorder, and post-traumatic stress disorder, are not prescribed when a client's *primary diagnosis* is specific phobia. It is difficult to justify use of these medications if the client is not otherwise depressed or does not experience anxiety apart from facing their particular phobic situation.

Common Problems

In the author's experience, there are four types of problems that are most likely to obstruct effective treatment. The first two were mentioned in the section on goals and limitations and are briefly recapitulated here:

1. Difficulties in simulating real-life exposure

2. Difficulties in obtaining a support person to accompany the client during exposure

3. Problems with client motivation and compliance with assigned homework

4. Resistance to recovery due to secondary gains

Difficulty Simulating Real-Life Exposure

For many types of specific phobias, particularly the situational ones, exposure can easily be conducted *in vivo*—in the actual situation. It is not so easy to do this with certain specific phobias. Exposure to live snakes or spiders may be difficult, for example, unless a trip to a local zoo can be arranged. Exposure to flying can be done once, but the repeated exposure necessary for mastery may be difficult and costly. It is impossible to conduct live exposure for phobias of rare natural events such as earthquakes, hurricanes, or tornadoes.

When real-life exposure is difficult or impossible, it is necessary to do extensive practice with imagery or other forms of simulated exposure. Audio and video tapes of the phobic object or situation can be helpful, and virtual exposure may be available in select places (see the preceding section, "Goals and Limitations"). The upshot of this is that expectations for *mastery* of a phobia are lower when repeated *in vivo* exposure is impractical. However, clients can be assured that significant gains in their ability to *cope* with their feared object or situation are possible through cognitive behavioral therapy utilizing imagery exposure alone. This has been demonstrated by the pioneering work of Joseph Wolpe with systematic desensitization as well as in my own experience treating phobias.

Difficulties in Obtaining a Support Person

For various reasons the therapist is not always able to accompany the client in undertaking exposure to a phobic situation. (For example, a therapist who cannot swim would not accompany a client who is fearful of deep water!) In such cases it is necessary to train a family member or friend of the client to be a support person. Such a person will be needed, in any case, to assist the client with practicing exposure between (and/or beyond) formal therapy sessions. The only exceptions are those cases when therapist and client mutually decide it would be most productive for the client to attempt exposure on their own. If the client wants to undertake exposure independently, this is encouraged.

When neither family nor friends are available to serve as an exposure support person, the therapist and client need to be resourceful in finding such a person. I have had success in having clients advertise at local colleges or in the newspaper to recruit an appropriate support person.

Motivation and Compliance with Homework

If a client is seriously depressed, then the depression needs to be treated effectively before undertaking cognitive behavioral treatment for a specific phobia. Other motivational problems may arise from personality disorders that predispose a client to be unmotivated or uncooperative in carrying out the tasks associated with exposure. For example, personality disorders involving severe authority conflict may render the client unwilling to follow instructions and complete assigned homework.

It is important to assess early on whether mood or personality factors are conducive to the client's willingness and ability to follow through with a highly structured form of therapy requiring compliance with weekly homework assignments.

Secondary Gains

Noncompliance with assigned homework may also be due to the operation of secondary gains—unconscious benefits the client receives from maintaining their phobic avoidance. An avoidance of public transportation for someone unable to drive may be difficult to overcome if the individual wishes to avoid having to work. No amount of desensitization is likely to help a phobia of injections if the person has other reasons for not trusting doctors or the medical establishment.

Sometimes resistance is due to a tacit agreement between the client and spouse or partner *not* to recover. If a husband is opposed to his wife overcoming a fear of flying because he doesn't trust her to be away from home without him, he will find a way to sabotage the treatment. Although interpersonal issues are less likely to play a role with specific phobia than with agoraphobia, they do sometimes have an impact.

In sum, when a client persistently fails to complete homework assignments, it is critical to explore the emotional reasons behind the resistance. If these issues cannot be resolved within one or two sessions, then you need to let the client know that the goal of overcoming their phobia in ten or so sessions is unattainable. Two alternatives are possible at this point: 1) the therapy contract can be renegotiated beyond ten sessions to focus on emotional issues and resistance first, and then the phobia, or 2) if the client is unable to do this, the therapy would best be terminated so as not to waste the client's time and money.

Closure and Follow-up

Therapy can be completed when both the client and therapist are satisfied that phobic avoidance has been fully overcome—the client no longer feels a need to avoid confronting their feared object or situation. Ideally, this means proceeding up through the "highest" (most challenging) step in the exposure hierarchy. As mentioned previously, there are two different standards of recovery: coping and mastery. Coping implies the ability to confront the phobic situation with mild to moderate levels of anxiety—and to rely on ad hoc use of medication if needed. Mastery implies the ability to handle the situation comfortably with little or no anxiety (and without the use of medication). It is important that therapist and client are clear about what standard of recovery is sought, and that therapy continue (barring financial constraints) until that standard is reached. As has been previously mentioned, full mastery may not always be attainable, and the client should be assisted in understanding the limitations of treatment where applicable.

To minimize relapse following completion of therapy, it is very useful to do a follow-up session approximately one month after the final session. Both during therapy and at the time of follow-up, it is important to reinforce the idea that *the client (wherever possible) needs to keep exposing themselves to the feared object or situation on a regular basis.* The benefits of exposure may fade if the client, through infrequency of practice, finds a way to start avoiding the situation again.

The client needs to be alert to signs of encroaching avoidance. This often begins with reliance on support that had previously been relinquished in the process of achieving a mastery level of recovery. For example, going back to using medication or a support person when the client had been able to do without them following treatment should be viewed as a warning sign of possible relapse. As soon as the client reverts to using old supports, it is time to increase the frequency of exposure to the situation until these supports once again become unnecessary. (See session 10 for additional discussion of relapse prevention.)

Finally, the last session is your opportunity to have the client complete the Program Satisfaction Questionnaire (next page). This instrument is useful in that it offers a way to precisely determine the client's views regarding the success of treatment. This is valuable for the therapist in terms of improving the techniques, and potentially important for managed care inquiries into the efficacy of the program.

Program Satisfaction Questionnaire (PSQ)

Please evaluate the therapy program you have just completed by answering the following questions. Circle the number that best reflects your opinion. Your honest answer, whether positive or negative, will give us feedback to make the program better.

1. How effective was the therapy program in helping you with your problem?

       1   2   3   4   5   6   7

   Not effective   *Moderately effective*   *Extremely effective*

2. How helpful were the homework and exercises in this therapy program?

       1   2   3   4   5   6   7

   Not helpful   *Moderately helpful*   *Extremely helpful*

3. Were the skills you learned in this therapy program useful for coping with your problem?

       1   2   3   4   5   6   7

   Not useful   *Moderately useful*   *Extremely useful*

4. Overall, how would you rate the quality of this therapy?

       1   2   3   4   5   6   7

   High quality   *Moderate quality*   *Low quality*

5. If someone with a similar problem to yours asked for recommendations, how would you describe the usefulness of this therapy program?

       1   2   3   4   5   6   7

   Not useful   *Moderately useful*   *Extremely useful*

6. If you could go back to remake your decision about this therapy program, would you do it again?

       1   2   3   4   5   6   7

   No definitely   *Uncertain*   *Yes definitely*

7. How successfully were your goals met by this therapy program?

       1   2   3   4   5   6   7

   Goals met   *Moderately successful* *Goals not met*
                     with goals

8. How would you rate your improvement in the symptoms that concerned you most?

       1   2   3   4   5   6   7

   Extremely improved *Moderately improved* *Not improved*

Session 1

Getting Started

Building an Initial Alliance

The initial task of the therapist in the first session is to build a therapeutic alliance. The ultimate success of the therapy depends on relationship elements that unfold during the first session. Clients need to feel heard, understood, and that the therapist is someone genuinely interested in helping.

After introductions, an opening question such as "How can I be of assistance to you?" will help elicit the client's goals for therapy. Then it is useful to proceed directly to taking a history. Asking the client to describe his or her current problem (in this case, a particular phobia) and its history immediately conveys the therapist's interest and concern. Although the history involves several focused questions, it is generally the *least directive* part of therapy. The purpose of history-taking is not only to obtain relevant information but to *build rapport*. Since clients so often need to ventilate feelings upon their first contact with a therapist, it is critical during the first twenty to thirty minutes to let them tell their story with few interruptions other than specific questions to elicit pertinent information.

Building rapport at this stage is best served in two ways: 1) active listening and 2) empathic validation of the client's feelings. The more the client feels heard and understood, the more likely they will tell the full story about their problem, including possible sources of inner resistance or interpersonal conflict that could potentially obstruct the course of therapy. Validating the client's feelings, especially expressed frustration and fear around facing a phobic situation, conveys that you as therapist are genuinely concerned and can appreciate the client's predicament. Certainly this helps to build trust. And trust on the client's part is a prerequisite for his or her willingness to engage in treatment and cooperate with directives and assigned homework.

The therapeutic stance in cognitive behavioral treatment is always collaborative (as opposed to authoritarian). As therapist you are there as a teacher and facilitator to help guide the client through a highly structured program that will eventuate in overcoming phobic avoidance. The responsibility for recovery always rests with the client; the therapist's role is to serve as a teacher, ally, and guide. It is important to convey (whatever the client's previous experience with therapy) that the orientation of cognitive behavioral therapy is *educational*. While there is a place in cognitive behavioral therapy for exploration of feelings and inner conflict, the primary focus is on learning new concepts and skills that will ensure mastery of anxiety and phobic avoidance.

Client Goals

After completing the initial assessment and history, it is critical to review with the client what their goal for therapy is. With specific phobia, the goal is usually straightforward—the client wishes to be able to face their phobic object or situation with minimal anxiety. This becomes the explicit goal of therapy unless, during the evaluation, the therapist has determined some other anxiety disorder or other behavioral disorder (e.g., dysthymia, substance abuse, hypochondriasis) is in fact the primary diagnosis.

Assessment

The assessment phase of the first session ordinarily takes thirty to forty-five minutes. For specific phobia, a semistructured interview is used which covers a series of topics, each with several questions. While it is important to address all the topics in the interview, in real life it is seldom necessary to proceed in a set order. As stated previously, history-taking should allow the client to tell their own story with minimal directiveness on the part of the therapist. This is a time to listen carefully and build rapport. Thus, the order in which the following six topics are covered will largely be determined by the client.

Phobia Evaluation Interview

History

1. When did your phobia first begin?

2. What circumstances do you feel caused you to develop your phobia?

3. Since you first developed your phobia, how has it progressed? Can you recall times when it got worse or better? What do you think might have contributed to making it worse or better?

Current Level of Impairment

4. Do you avoid your phobia (object, situation) altogether? Have there been times when you have faced it? Were these confrontations voluntary (e.g., you decided to try flying) or involuntary (e.g., you went through an earthquake)? What happened when you tried to (or had to) deal with your phobia in the past?

5. Do you occasionally attempt to confront your phobia at present? If so, what happened most recently?

6. Can you confront your phobia (object/situation) if you have a support person with you? If so, how much more can you do with a support person vs. being alone?

7. Have you had panic attacks when you faced your phobia? (A panic attack means your anxiety reached a level where you felt out of control, with pronounced symptoms such as dizziness, shakiness, heart palpitations, or extreme urgency to leave the situation.) How frequently has panic occurred (every time, sometimes, only on one or two occasions)? On a scale of 1 to 10, how intense has been your experience of panic? ("1" is a state of anxiety where you are just beginning to feel a little out of control, along with a desire to leave the situation, and "10" is a state of being overwhelmed with fear to the point of intense apprehension or terror.)

8. Describe the anxiety you experience when you anticipate facing your phobia (object/situation). At what point do you begin to feel anxious?

   • Mere mention of your phobia (object or situation)
   • Someone talks about your phobic situation
   • Thinking about your phobic situation
   • Seeing a picture of the situation
   • Visualizing your phobic situation
   • Deciding that you will actually face the situation at some time in the future
      a. One month before you confront the situation
      b. One week before you confront the situation
      c. One day before you confront the situation
      d. One hour before you confront the situation
      e. One minute before you confront the situation
      f. Entering or directly exposing yourself to the situation

Prior Treatment

9. Have you sought professional help for your phobia in the past? When and with whom? What kind of treatment did you receive? What was the outcome of this treatment? Have you sought professional help for other reasons apart from your phobia?

Coping Strategies

10. How have you tried to cope with your phobia on your own? If you have attempted to (or had to) face your fear, what coping strategies did you devise to get you through? How well do you feel these strategies worked?

Medication

11. Have you used medication to help you face your phobia? What was the medication? Did you use it regularly (every day) for a period of time or only when you confronted your phobic situation? Do you remember what dose you took? Who prescribed the medication? What effect do you think the medication had? (It is useful to note whether the client has been taking a benzodiazepine tranquilizer such as Xanax or Klonopin for more than a year. Long-term use or escalation of the dose may indicate possible benzodiazepine dependence, which can interfere with the ultimate effectiveness of exposure.)

Current Resources

12. How strongly motivated are you to overcome your phobia? Are you willing to spend up to an hour per day, five days per week, doing homework assignments that will enable you to master your phobia? Are you willing to risk experiencing some anxiety when doing real-life exposure to overcome your fear?

13. Does your spouse or partner (family, friends, roommates, etc.) understand your phobia? Do you think they will support you in your efforts to overcome it? Do you think anyone might have a vested interest in your not getting better? (Anyone who might knowingly or unknowingly want you to remain as you are?)

14. It may be necessary to have someone accompany you when you first start to confront your fear. Do you have a family member or friend whom you think would be willing to accompany you in doing exposure practice between your weekly therapy sessions? Do you think this person would support you at your own pace and not push you during your practice?

15. Do you have the time and financial resources to follow through with treatment to completion (approximately ten weekly sessions with daily homework assignments between sessions)?

Sharing Your Conclusions

After the assessment, let the client know whether they are dealing only with a specific phobia, or another disorder primarily. In the latter instance, the client then needs to be apprised of this and told that their specific phobia can most effectively be treated only if the more primary disorder is dealt with first. When specific phobia *is* the primary diagnosis, it is useful to tell the client so. Knowing that their problem has a name gives most clients a specific context for understanding what is going on with them a little better.

With the problem named and the goal of treatment explicit, the therapist is ready to begin explaining the treatment.

Treatment Recommendations

The last ten to fifteen minutes of the initial session should be devoted to giving the client both an explanation of the treatment interventions and their rationale. By explaining treatment, you let the client know that you have a plan. Clearly this helps to: 1) increase the client's trust in the therapy and the therapist and 2) create a positive expectation that therapy can be effective. Positive expectancy of a favorable outcome is a key ingredient in motivating the client to engage in therapy. For clients who have previously received only insight-oriented talk therapy in response to their phobic issues, the description of focused, cognitive behavioral interventions can be a welcome relief. Beyond merely describing interventions, it is important to help the client understand their rationale—how and why they work. When clients understand the *reason* for behavioral interventions such as systematic desensitization and exposure, they are certainly more likely to be motivated to carry out weekly homework assignments. Understanding the rationale for interventions also adds to the client's expectancy of a favorable outcome. They can leave the initial session with some hope that therapy can truly help them.

I have found it useful to explain treatment as having two stages: 1) learning to manage anxiety that can arise before or during confronting a phobia, and 2) actually facing their phobia *gradually* through a series of small, incremental steps. The first two or three sessions of therapy are devoted to breathing retraining, relaxation training, and anxiety (panic) management strategies so that the client will have skills to handle any anxiety that comes up during the course of exposure. With these skills in place, the remaining sessions of therapy are devoted to the process of confronting their fear, breaking that process down into a series of manageable steps. While the client may feel it is improbable or impossible that they could fly or receive a hypodermic injection at the outset of therapy, it is important to provide reassurance that they can—if the problem is broken down into a sufficient number of small, incremental steps. Systematic desensitization allows them to face their phobic situation in imagery first, before dealing with it in real life. Then, when they are ready to undertake real-life exposure, the process will be broken down into a number of steps to make it manageable. Moreover, they will have their anxiety management skills, a support person and, if necessary, even medication to assist them in negotiating each step. What may seem quite difficult at the outset will not be so bad with all of these resources available.

Sample Explanation

An explanation of therapy might go something like this:

"During the first two or three sessions we'll focus on learning some basic relaxation and anxiety management skills. These include abdominal breathing, progressive muscle relaxation, and specific anxiety coping skills. All of this will increase your confidence and motivation when, later in therapy, you begin to actually confront your fear of _____. You'll have a chance to practice these skills to a high level of mastery before you actually confront your phobic situation. We'll also focus on any mistaken beliefs and unhelpful self-talk you have around your phobia.

"When you think about facing your fear of _____, you probably start to get anxious. That anxiety, called anticipatory anxiety, is mostly due to unhelpful, frightening thoughts you have about your phobia. Usually there are two kinds of anxiety-provoking thoughts. First, there are those which overestimate the odds of something undesirable happening when you face your fear. These overestimating thoughts usually begin with a 'What if,' for example: 'What if I panic and feel trapped on the plane?' 'What if I faint while getting a shot?' or 'What if the elevator stops between floors and I'm trapped?' The other kind of unhelpful thoughts are those where you underestimate your ability to cope with your phobic situation, for example: 'There is no way I can ever do that,' or 'If I panicked, I'd be at a total loss about what to do.' You can learn to recognize, challenge, and counter unhelpful self-talk. After a while, this will help you to change your attitude—the way you look at facing your phobia.

"During the second part of therapy you will begin to actually confront your fear of _____. Ultimately, there is no other way to overcome a phobia except to face it. However, doing so will not be so bad as you might think, because we'll break down the process of confronting your fear into small, manageable steps. Before facing your fear in real life, you will face it in imagery. You'll learn a process called 'imagery desensitization' where you visualize yourself confronting what you fear in a series of incremental steps. Learning to visualize your phobic situation without anxiety will help you to manage confronting it in real life. When you finally begin to approach your phobic situation in real life—what is called *exposure*—that, too, will be broken down into a series of small, manageable steps. You may experience some anxiety during exposure, but it's unlikely to ever get out of hand. You'll have a support person to accompany you during each step of the exposure process. You'll learn to back off from exposure—what is called *retreat*—if you experience excessive anxiety and will only return to the situation when your anxiety subsides.

"It's useful during exposure for you to have mild levels of anxiety, but not high levels. Yet, it's unlikely that your anxiety will ever reach a high level, for these four reasons: 1) you'll have a support person go with you, 2) you'll face your fear in small, incremental steps, 3) you'll learn to back off temporarily if your anxiety becomes too high, and 4) you'll have a variety of relaxation and anxiety management skills at your disposal.

"If necessary we can also use medication. So I would like to reassure you at this point that you'll be able to gradually face your phobia without high or distressing levels of anxiety. In fact, that is the whole point of this therapy."

Following an explanation of therapy along these lines, it is important to ask whether the client has any questions. In the interest of time, detailed explanations of specific interventions such as cognitive restructuring or exposure should be deferred to later sessions.

It is important next to communicate to the client the importance of assigned homework. This might be conveyed as follows:

"A critical part of this therapy is the homework assignments that I'll be asking you to do each week. For the therapy to be effective, you need to learn a variety of skills that require some practice at home between sessions. I'll teach you the skills here in therapy, but to master them you need to practice them on a daily basis at home. In short, your ability to overcome your phobia will depend largely on whether you do the assigned homework. I'd like you to be aware of this at the outset. If you feel you're willing to make a commitment to doing homework assignments that will require thirty minutes to an hour of your time, five days a week, then we can go forward. If you feel you aren't ready or motivated to make that kind of commitment, then we should defer treatment until you feel you're ready. I want you to receive fully what this therapy can offer you. Not to do so would not be a good use of your time and money."

Following a statement along these lines, it is important to explore any feelings or concerns the client has about homework. Most clients will agree to the idea of homework at the time of the first session. Compliance in later sessions is another matter.

Expectations For Therapy

Clients generally want to know how long therapy will take, so it is useful at this point to let them know that the treatment for their phobia will require a minimum of ten weeks and possibly longer. If the client's phobia lends itself easily to exposure, then they can expect to attain a "mastery" level of recovery—i.e., the ability to negotiate their phobic situation with little or no anxiety. If their particular phobia does *not* easily allow for exposure (e.g. fear of tornadoes or throwing up), then the client should receive a realistic statement of treatment expectations. While an increased ability to cope with the situation is certainly likely, full mastery may not be feasible.

Summary of Session

The therapy hour can close with a brief summary of the first session. A possible summary might be:

"Our purpose here is for you to learn specific strategies and skills for overcoming your phobia of _____. The process will take about ten (or more) weeks, and you'll actually face your phobia through a series of small, incremental steps. However, before doing so, you'll have learned a number of skills to handle any anxiety that comes up. Each week you will receive homework assignments to practice the skills learned in therapy at home. If you make a commitment to do the homework, you'll very likely overcome your phobia. The methods I would like you to learn really do work, if you make the time and effort to do your part."

Feedback from Client

After summarizing the session, it's very important to ask the client if they have any questions, and allow a small amount of time for answering them.

Homework Assignment

Homework for the first session is usually a reading assignment to help the client understand the nature of their problem and the first stages of treatment. This is the point to give them the *Client Manual for Overcoming Specific Phobia*, which describes the nature and rationale of cognitive behavioral therapy in an accessible language. They may also be referred to chapter 4 of *The Anxiety and Phobia Workbook* (1995), which describes abdominal breathing and relaxation strategies to be taught the following week.

Session 2

Breathing and Relaxation Techniques

Monitoring of Current Status

The second and each subsequent session can begin by asking the client whether any significant concerns or issues have come up since the preceding session (either related to the therapy or otherwise). Before going on with the agenda for the session, the client needs to express about any pressing concerns. And if a personal crisis has occurred, some or even all of the session may need to focus on addressing the client's feelings before returning to the regular treatment protocol. A major event such as a death in the client's family usually means behavioral goals will be put on hold for a few weeks. Responding empathically to major life changes takes precedence over treating a specific phobia. Fortunately, in most cases, the client's concerns from the preceding week can be addressed in a few minutes.

Agenda

Next, it is important to summarize the interventions to be covered in the current session. Reiterate the reason why these interventions are useful in helping the client to overcome his or her particular phobia.

In session 2, the three interventions covered are abdominal breathing (breathing retraining), progressive muscle relaxation, and visualizing a peaceful scene. The purpose of these interventions is to give clients effective strategies for reducing both

1) anxiety in response to imaginal or *in vivo* exposure, and 2) anticipatory anxiety in advance of facing their phobia.

The client should actually practice all three of the following interventions *in session* before being given homework to practice them at home.

Review of Homework

The next task is to ask the client about how they did with the homework assignment from the previous session. Any problems encountered in completing homework need to be discussed and hopefully resolved. When the client fails to do assigned homework, motivational and/or resistance issues should be addressed. Guidelines for "troubleshooting" common types of problems that arise in carrying out behavioral assignments will be presented in the "Review of Homework" section of each session.

By asking the client about homework near the beginning of each session, the message is repeatedly given that homework is a vital part of the treatment.

Concepts and Skills

Please note that interventions in this and following sessions are worded as though you, as therapist, were explaining them to the client.

Abdominal Breathing

Psychoeducation

Your breathing directly reflects the level of tension you carry in your body. Under tension, your breathing usually becomes shallow and rapid, and occurs high in the chest. When relaxed, you breathe more fully, more deeply, and from your abdomen. It's difficult to be tense and to breathe from your abdomen at the same time.

Some of the benefits of abdominal breathing include:

- Increased oxygen supply to the brain and musculature.

- Stimulation of the parasympathetic nervous system. This branch of your autonomic nervous system promotes a state of calmness and quiescence. It works in a fashion exactly opposite to the sympathetic branch of your nervous system, which stimulates a state of emotional arousal and the very physiological reactions underlying panic and anxiety.

- Greater feelings of connectedness between mind and body. Anxiety and worry tend to keep you "up in your head." A few minutes of deep abdominal breathing will help bring you down into your whole body.

- Improved concentration. If your mind is racing, it's difficult to focus your attention. Abdominal breathing will help to quiet your mind.

- Abdominal breathing by itself can trigger deep relaxation.

Abdominal breathing means breathing fully from your abdomen or from the bottom of your lungs. It is exactly the reverse of the way you breathe when you're anxious or tense, which is typically shallow and high in your chest. If you're breathing from your abdomen, you can place your hand on your stomach and see it actually *rise* each time you inhale.

Skill Building

To practice abdominal breathing, observe the following steps:

1. Place one hand on your abdomen right beneath your rib cage, preferably while sitting or lying down.

2. Inhale slowly and deeply through your nose into the bottom of your lungs (the lowest point down in your lungs you can reach). Your chest should move only slightly, while your stomach rises, pushing your hand up.

3. When you've inhaled fully, pause for a moment and then exhale fully through your nose or your mouth. Be sure to exhale fully. As you exhale, just let yourself go and imagine your entire body going loose and limp.

4. In order to fully relax, take and release ten abdominal breaths. Try to keep your breathing *smooth* and *regular* throughout, without gulping in air or exhaling suddenly. It will help to slow down your breathing if you slowly count to four ("one, two, three, four") on the inhale and then slowly count to four again on the exhale. Use the one through four count for at least the first week of practicing abdominal breathing.

5. After you've become proficient in slowing down your breathing, you can drop the one through four count if you wish. At this point, try counting backward from twenty down to one, one count after each exhale. That is, after the first exhale count "twenty," after the next "nineteen," and so on down to zero. Remember to keep your breath slow and regular throughout, inhaling through your nose, and exhaling through your nose or mouth.

6. Continue to practice abdominal breathing for five minutes. If you start to feel light-headed at any time, stop for thirty seconds and then start up again.

7. Practice abdominal breathing for *five minutes every day, three times per day, for at least two weeks.* If possible, find regular times each day to do this so that your breathing exercise becomes a habit. With practice you can learn in a short period of time to slow down the physiological reactions underlying anxiety.

Once you feel you've gained some mastery in the use of this technique, apply it whenever you feel anxious about facing your phobia. With continued practice, you'll be able to use abdominal breathing to reduce anxiety you have in advance of facing your fear (anticipatory anxiety) as well as anxiety that may come up when you're actually in the situation.

Progressive Muscle Relaxation

Psychoeducation

Progressive muscle relaxation is a systematic technique for achieving a deep state of relaxation. It was developed by Dr. Edmund Jacobson more than fifty years ago. Dr. Jacobson discovered that a muscle could be relaxed by first tensing it for a few seconds and then releasing it. Tensing and releasing various muscle groups throughout the body produces a deep state of relaxation, which Dr. Jacobson found capable of relieving a variety of conditions, from high blood pressure to colitis.

Progressive muscle relaxation is especially helpful for people whose anxiety is strongly associated with muscle tension. This is what often leads you to say that you are "uptight" or "tense." You may experience chronic tightness in your shoulders and neck, which can be effectively relieved by progressive muscle relaxation.

Progressive muscle relaxation can help you reduce anticipatory anxiety that comes up when you think of facing your phobia. It is also useful in practicing imagery desensitization, which you'll learn in a later session.

Skill Building

Progressive muscle relaxation involves tensing and relaxing sixteen different muscle groups of the body. The idea is to tense each muscle group hard (not so hard that you strain, however) for about ten seconds, and then to let go of it suddenly. You then give yourself fifteen to twenty seconds to relax, noticing how the muscle group feels when relaxed in contrast to how it felt when tensed, before going on to the next group of muscles. You might also say to yourself "I am relaxing," "Letting go," "Let the tension flow away," or any other relaxing phrase during each relaxation period between successive muscle groups. Throughout the exercise, maintain your focus on your muscles. When your attention wanders, bring it back to the particular muscle group you're working on. The guidelines below describe progressive muscle relaxation in detail:

- Make sure you are in a setting that is quiet and comfortable.

- It's preferable to practice on an empty stomach—before or one hour after a meal.

- It's preferable to be seated in a recliner or lying down, with your head supported.

- When you tense a particular muscle group, do so vigorously, without straining, for seven to ten seconds. You may want to count "one-thousand-one," "one-thousand-two," and so on, as a way of marking off seconds.

- Concentrate on what is happening. Feel the buildup of tension in each particular muscle group. It is often helpful to visualize the particular muscle group being tensed.

- When you release the muscles, do so abruptly and then relax, enjoying the sudden feeling of limpness. Allow the relaxation to develop for at least fifteen to twenty seconds before going on to the next group of muscles.

- Allow all the *other* muscles in your body to remain as relaxed as possible while tensing a particular muscle group.

- Tense and relax each muscle group once. If a particular area feels especially tight, you can tense and relax it two or three times, waiting about twenty seconds between each cycle.

Once you are comfortably supported in a quiet place, follow the detailed instructions below:

1. To begin, take three deep abdominal breaths, inhaling and exhaling slowly through your nose each time. As you exhale, imagine that tension throughout your body is flowing away.

2. Clench your fists. Hold for seven to ten seconds and then release for fifteen to twenty seconds. *Use these same time intervals for all other muscle groups.*

3. Tighten your biceps by drawing your forearms up toward your shoulders and "making a muscle" with both arms. Hold . . . and then relax.

4. Tighten your triceps—the muscles on the undersides of your upper arms—by extending your arms out straight and locking your elbows. Hold . . . and then relax.

5. Tense the muscles in your forehead by raising your eyebrows as far as you can. Hold . . . and then relax. Imagine your forehead muscles becoming smooth and limp as they relax.

6. Tense the muscles around your eyes by clenching your eyelids tightly shut. Hold . . . and then relax. Imagine sensations of deep relaxation spreading all around the area of your eyes.

7. Tighten your jaws by opening your mouth widely so that you stretch the muscles around the hinges of your jaw. Hold . . . and then relax. Let your lips part and allow your jaw to hang loose.

8. Tighten the muscles in the back of your neck by pulling your head way back, as if you were going to touch your head to your back (be gentle with this muscle group to avoid injury). Focus only on tensing the muscles in your neck. Hold . . . and then relax. Since this area is often especially tight, it's good to do the tense-relax cycle twice.

9. Take a few deep breaths and tune in to the weight of your head sinking into whatever surface it's resting on.

10. Tighten your shoulders by raising them up as if you were going to touch your ears. Hold . . . and then relax.

11. Tighten the muscles around your shoulder blades by pushing back your shoulder blades as if you were going to touch them together. Hold the tension in your shoulder blades . . . and then relax. Since this area is often especially tense, you might repeat the tense-relax sequence twice.

12. Tighten the muscles of your chest by taking in a deep breath. Hold for up to ten seconds . . . and then release slowly. Imagine any excess tension in your chest flowing away with the exhalation.

13. Tighten your stomach muscles by sucking your stomach in. Hold . . . and then release. Imagine a wave of relaxation spreading through your abdomen.

14. Tighten your lower back muscles by arching your back. (You can omit this exercise if you have lower back pain.) Hold . . . and then relax.

15. Tighten your buttock muscles by pulling them together. Hold . . . and then relax. Imagine the muscles in your hips going loose and limp.

16. Squeeze the muscles in your thighs all the way down to your knees. You will probably have to tighten your buttocks along with your thighs, since the thigh muscles attach at the pelvis. Hold . . . and then relax. Feel your thigh muscles smoothing out and relaxing completely.

17. Tighten your calf muscles by pulling your toes toward you (flex carefully to avoid cramps). Hold . . . and then relax.

18. Tighten your feet by curling your toes downward. Hold . . . and then relax.

19. Mentally scan your body for any residual tension. If a particular area remains tense, repeat one or two tense-relax cycles for that group of muscles.

20. Now imagine a wave of relaxation gradually spreading throughout your body, starting at your head and slowly penetrating every muscle group all the way down to your toes.

The entire progressive muscle relaxation sequence should take you twenty to thirty minutes the first time. With practice you may decrease the time needed to fifteen to twenty minutes.

You might want to record the above exercises on an audio cassette to expedite your early practice sessions. Or you may wish to obtain a professionally made tape of progressive muscle relaxation. Some people always prefer to use a tape, while others have the exercises so well learned after a few weeks of practice that they prefer doing them from memory. (Note: The therapist may opt to record instructions for progressive muscle relaxation on tape while the client is relaxing in session.)

It's important to practice progressive muscle relaxation at least once per day. Twice per day is preferable if you feel anxious much of the time; otherwise once per day is sufficient. Try to practice at approximately the same time each day so that you can develop the habit more easily.

Remember—regular practice of progressive muscle relaxation once a day will reduce anticipatory anxiety that may arise when systematically exposing yourself to your phobic situation. Progressive muscle relaxation is also useful to help you relax before doing imagery desensitization, which you'll learn in three weeks.

Visualizing a Peaceful Scene

Psychoeducation

After completing progressive muscle relaxation, it's helpful to visualize yourself in the midst of a peaceful scene. Progressive muscle relaxation addresses particular groups of muscles; imagining yourself in a very peaceful setting can give you a global sense of relaxation that frees you from anxious thoughts. The peaceful scene can be a quiet beach, a stream in the mountains, or a calm lake. Or it can be your bedroom or a cozy fireside on a cold winter night. Don't restrict yourself to reality: you can imagine, if you want to, floating on a cloud or flying on a magic carpet. The important thing is to visualize the scene in sufficient detail so that it completely absorbs your attention. Allowing yourself to be absorbed in a peaceful scene will deepen your state of relaxation, giving you actual physiological results. Your muscular tension lessens, your heart rate slows down, your breathing deepens, your capillaries open up and warm your hands and feet, and so on. A relaxing visualization constitutes a light form of self-hypnosis.

Skill Building

Here are two examples of peaceful scenes. (The therapist may want to give the client a handout with these two scripts, though they are reproduced in the client manual.)

❖

You're walking along a beautiful, deserted beach. You are barefoot and can feel the firm white sand beneath your feet as you walk along the margin of the sea. You can hear the sound of the surf as the waves ebb and flow. The sound is hypnotic, relaxing you more and more. The water is a beautiful turquoise blue flecked with whitecaps far out where the waves are cresting. Near the horizon you can see a small sailboat gliding smoothly along. The sound of the waves breaking on the shore lulls you deeper and deeper into relaxation. You draw in the fresh, salty smell of the air with each breath. Your skin glows with the warmth of the sun. You can feel a gentle breeze against your cheek and ruffling your hair. Taking in the whole scene, you feel very calm and at ease.

❖

You're snuggled in your sleeping bag. Daylight is breaking in the forest. You can feel the rays of the sun beginning to warm your face. The dawn sky stretches above you in pastel shades of pink and orange. You can smell the fresh, pine fragrance of the surrounding woods. Nearby you can hear the rushing waters of a mountain stream. The crisp, cool morning air is refreshing and invigorating. You're feeling very cozy, comfortable, and secure.

Note that these scenes are described in language that appeals to the senses of sight, hearing, touch, and smell. Using multisensory words helps to make the scene more compelling, enabling you to experience it as if you were actually there. The whole point of imagining a peaceful scene is to transport yourself from your normal state of restless thinking into an altered state of deep relaxation.

You may want to design your own peaceful scene. Be sure to describe it in vivid detail, appealing to as many senses as possible. It may help to answer the following questions: What does the scene look like? What colors are prominent? What sounds are present? What time of day is it? What is the temperature? What are you touching or in physical contact with in the scene? What does the air smell like? Are you alone or with somebody else?

Just as with progressive muscle relaxation, you may wish to record your peaceful scene on tape so that you can conjure it up without effort. You might want to record your scene on the same tape following the instructions for progressive muscle relaxation.

Use the script below to introduce your peaceful scene when you make your own recording (this script could be included on the handout previously described, and is also in the client manual).

❖

... Just think of relaxing every muscle in your body, from the top of your head to the tips of your toes.

... As you exhale, imagine releasing any remaining tension from your body, mind, or thoughts ... just let that stress go.

... And with every breath you inhale, feel your body drifting down deeper ... down deeper into total relaxation.

... And now imagine going to your peaceful scene.... Imagine your special place as vividly as possible, as if you were really there. (Insert your peaceful scene.)

... You are very comfortable in your beautiful place, and there is no one to disturb you.... This is the most peaceful place in the world for you.... Just imagine yourself there, feeling a sense of peace flow through you and a sense of well-being. Enjoy these positive feelings.... Allow them to grow stronger and stronger.

... And remember, anytime you wish, you can return to this special place by just taking time to relax.

... These peaceful and positive feelings of relaxation can grow stronger and stronger each time you choose to relax.

Once you have imagined your own ideal peaceful scene, practice returning to it every time you do progressive muscle relaxation, deep breathing, or any other relaxation technique. This will help to reinforce the scene in your mind. After a while it will be so solidly established that you will be able to return to it on the spur of the moment—whenever you wish to calm yourself and turn off anxious thinking. This technique is one of the quickest and most effective tools you can use to counter ongoing anxiety or stress during the day.

Summary of Session

Briefly summarize the material covered in the session.

Feedback from Client

This is a chance for the client to express any concerns or comments they may have about the session, and to ask questions.

Homework

Homework given for session 2 is as follows:

1. Practice abdominal breathing for five minutes three times per day.

2. Practice progressive muscle relaxation for twenty to twenty-five minutes at least once per day, having someone read the instructions or using a tape with instructions prerecorded.

3. Practice visualizing a peaceful scene after each occasion when you practice progressive muscle relaxation. Work on visualizing the scene in as much detail as possible. Use the scenes in your client manual or feel free to make up your own.

Session 2—Main Points

- Explain the nature and benefits of abdominal breathing as a method for managing anxiety.

- Teach the client to do abdominal breathing and have them practice for two to three minutes in session.

- Explain progressive muscle relaxation (PMR) as a deep relaxation technique as well as the foundation for imagery desensitization (which will be taught in session 5).

- If time permits, have the client practice PMR in session. Otherwise encourage the client to make a tape of the detailed instructions for PMR (page 13 of the client manual), or provide the client with a prerecorded tape.

- Have the client identify a peaceful scene and practice visualizing it in session. A script for the peaceful scene should follow instructions for PMR on the client's relaxation tape.

- Assign homework.

Session 3

Restructuring Phobic Self-Talk

Monitoring of Current Status

(as in session 2)

Agenda

This week focuses on learning to identify and counter unproductive self-talk which contributes to the client's phobia. Specific phobias involve more than merely conditioned fear reactions to particular situations. The more anticipatory anxiety the client has when thinking about his or her phobia, the larger the role fearful self-talk likely plays in aggravating the fear. By addressing unhelpful cognitions, the intensity of the client's fear toward their phobic situation can be reduced.

Review of Homework

Ask the client how their practice with abdominal breathing and progressive muscle relaxation went. Did they make time to practice these techniques on a daily basis? If they didn't practice, ask for self-talk that came up when they thought about home-work but decided not to do it. Identify common excuses like: "I didn't have the time," "I didn't have the discipline," "I don't see how this can help," and assist the client in confronting their own resistance. Reiterate the critical importance of doing homework in order to benefit from therapy.

Some common problems that may arise in practicing abdominal breathing and progressive muscle relaxation, along with remedial interventions, are as follows:

1. The client is dizzy or lightheaded when practicing abdominal breathing.

   Slow down the pace of breathing:

   - Inhale through the nose—not the mouth.

   - Make breathing slightly less deep by counting to two or three instead of four on the inhale and exhale (keep breathing pace slow).

   - Stop periodically and do your normal breathing pattern until light-headedness goes away; then resume abdominal breathing.

2. Doing abdominal breathing makes the client more anxious.

   - If anxiety is in response to dizziness or lightheadedness, try the inter-ventions in number 1.

   - Otherwise, phase in abdominal breathing gradually. Start with one-minute practice periods and gradually increase the duration, one minute at a time, up to five minutes.

   - Do abdominal breathing sitting up, instead of lying down.

   - If emotionally-charged material was evoked by doing abdominal breathing, this needs to be explored in session.

3. The client reports that he or she cannot get sufficiently relaxed during pro-gressive muscle relaxation.

   - Do not strain when tensing muscles.

   - Hold tension longer before releasing it in each muscle group.

   - Pause for longer periods of time between relaxing one muscle group and proceeding to tense the next.

Some clients simply do not like progressive muscle relaxation. They find the tense-relax process too effortful or they are already so tense that the process does not have much impact. Such clients should be advised to practice a *passive* muscle re-laxation technique (consisting of a series of direct suggestions to relax various mus-cles groups) or guided visualizations that induce relaxation. Scripts for these alternate forms of relaxation can be found in chapter 12 of *The Anxiety and Phobia Workbook* (1995) or on the author's tape series relating to eight different specific pho-bias (see appendix 3).

Concepts and Skills

Changing Self-Talk That Perpetuates Specific Phobias

Psychoeducation

Three factors tend to perpetuate fears and phobias: 1) sensitization, 2) avoidance, and 3) negative, distorted self-talk. A phobia develops when you become sensitized to a particular situation, object, or event—in other words, when anxiety becomes conditioned or associated with that situation, object, or event. If panic suddenly arises while you happen to be flying or riding an elevator, you may start feeling anxious every time you're in either of these situations. Becoming *sensitized* means that the mere presence of—or even thinking about—a situation may be enough to trigger anxiety automatically.

After sensitization occurs, you may start to *avoid* the situation. Repeated avoidance is very rewarding, because it saves you from having to feel any anxiety. Avoidance is the most powerful way to hold on to a phobia, because it prevents you from ever learning that you can handle the situation. We will deal with the sensitization and avoidance aspects of your phobia starting next week.

The third factor that perpetuates fears and phobias is distorted self-talk. The more *worry* and *anticipatory anxiety* you experience about something you fear, the more likely you are involved in unconstructive self-talk connected with that fear. You may also have negative *images* about what could happen if you had to face what you fear, or about your worst fears coming true. Both the negative self-talk and negative images serve to perpetuate your fear, guaranteeing that you remain afraid. They also undermine your confidence about ever getting over your fear. By reducing your negative self-talk and negative images, you'll be more likely to overcome your avoidance and confront your phobia.

Phobias come in many forms, but the nature of fearful self-talk is always the same. Whether you are afraid of crossing bridges, heights, or getting a shot, the types of distorted thinking which perpetuate these fears are the same. There are *two* basic distortions:

1. *Overestimating a Negative Outcome:* overestimating the odds of something bad happening. Most of the time your worries consist of "what if" statements which overestimate a particular negative outcome. For example, "What if I panic and lose complete control of myself?" "What if the plane crashes?" "What if I flunk the exam and have to drop out of school?"

2. *Underestimating Your Ability to Cope:* not recognizing or acknowledging your ability to cope with the situation, even if a negative outcome did, in fact, occur. This underestimation of your ability to cope is usually implicit in your overestimating thoughts.

If you take any fear and examine the negative thinking that contributes to maintaining that fear, you'll probably find these two distortions. To the extent that you can overcome these distortions with more reality-based thinking, the fear will tend to diminish. In essence, you can define fear as *the unreasonable overestimation of some threat, coupled with an underestimation of your ability to cope.*

Here are some examples of how the two types of distortions operate with various fears. In each example, both types of distorted thoughts are identified. Then the distortions are challenged in each case and modified with more appropriate, reality-based counterstatements.

Example 1: Fear of Driving on a Freeway

Overestimating Thoughts: "What if I can't handle the car? What if my attention wanders and I lose control of the car? What if I cause an accident and kill someone?"

Underestimating Your Ability to Cope: "I couldn't cope if I lost control of the car, especially if I got into an accident. What would I say to a policeman—that I'm phobic? I wouldn't be able to start driving again if I got stopped for a ticket. I couldn't live with myself if I caused physical injury to another person—and I know I couldn't face life myself in a wheelchair."

It's possible to refute each of these types of distorted thinking with questions and counterstatements. Examples follow below:

Challenging Your Overestimating Thoughts: With overestimating thoughts, the appropriate question is: *"Viewing the situation objectively, what are the odds of the negative outcome actually happening?"*

In the case of the previous example, the question is, "If I did panic while driving, what are the actual odds that I would lose control of the car?"

Here is an example of a counterstatement you might use: "It's unlikely that having a panic attack would cause me to lose complete control of the car. The moment I felt my anxiety coming on, I could pull over to the shoulder on the side of the road and stop. If there weren't any shoulders, I could slow down in the right lane, perhaps to forty-five mph, put my flashers on, and keep a grip on myself until I reached the nearest exit. Once I got off the freeway, my panic would begin to subside."

Challenging Your Underestimation of Your Ability to Cope: Countering the idea that you couldn't cope often takes place in the process of answering overestimating thoughts with a more objective appraisal. However, the process isn't complete until you actually identify and list specific ways in which you would cope. The operative question is: *"If the worst happened, what could I do to cope?"* In the above example, some possible coping strategies might include: "If I did have a panic attack on the freeway, I would cope by getting off the highway immediately or driving slowly to the nearest exist and getting off. In the very unlikely case that I actually caused an accident, I would still cope. I would exchange names and addresses with other parties involved. If my car were undriveable, the police would likely drive me to a place where I would call to have the car towed. It would be a very unpleasant experience, to say the least; but, realistically, I would continue to function. I've functioned in emergencies in the past, and I could function in this case, if I weren't injured. Even given the unlikely possibility that I were injured, I wouldn't 'go crazy' or 'totally lose it.' I would simply wait until the paramedics came and took charge of the situation."

Example 2: Fear of Flying

Overestimating Thoughts: "With my luck, the plane might get into bad weather. What if it *did* go down?" "Even if the plane makes it, what if I get claustrophobic sitting there for two hours? What if I panic?"

Challenging: "What are the realistic odds that I'll be in a plane crash?" "What is the actual likelihood that I'll panic while aboard the plane? If I do panic, what are the realistic odds I'll feel horribly or irreparably trapped?"

Counterstatements: "The realistic odds of my plane crashing, no matter what the weather or turbulence encountered, is one in seven million." (This is actually the case.) "I'm less likely to panic during the flight if I have a support person with me, or if I get up several times from my seat to walk in the aisle. The perception of being trapped is an illusion based on the fact that I have a lot of energy without the ability to release it through activity."

Underestimating Ability to Cope: (Imagining the worst) "There is no way I could cope if the plane went down." "I don't see how I could cope with panicking and the feeling of being trapped. I'd lose control and freak out."

Challenging: "If the worst happened, what could I actually do?"

Coping Strategies: "Probably no one would cope very well if the plane went down. However, there would be very little time to think about it—it would all be over before I had time to react for very long. Also, I would feel no pain because I would be unconscious before I had any time to perceive physical pain. I can resist the temptation to imagine this scenario by reminding myself of the odds of being in a plane crash. I would have to fly every single day for nineteen thousand years before my 'number would be up.'

Suppose I did panic midflight. I could use any of several anxiety management strategies to handle it—i.e., abdominal breathing, walking up and down the aisle, coping statements, talking to my support person (or calling someone on a cellular phone, if available). I could even take medication, if necessary. I'm confident that *something* would help me to feel better after a few minutes."

Example 3: Fear of Contracting a Serious Illness

Overestimating Thoughts: "I have no energy and feel tired all the time. Maybe I'm developing cancer and don't know it!"

Challenging: "What are the odds that symptoms of low energy and fatigue mean that I'm developing cancer?"

Counterstatements: "Symptoms of fatigue and low energy can be indicative of all kinds of physical and psychological conditions, including a low-grade virus, anemia, adrenal exhaustion or hypothyroidism, depression, and food allergies, to name a few. There are many possible explanations of my condition, and I don't have any specific symptoms that would indicate cancer. So the odds of my fatigue and low energy indicating cancer are very low."

Underestimating Ability To Cope: "If I were diagnosed with cancer, that would be the end. I couldn't take it. I'd be better off ending things quickly and killing myself."

Challenging: "If the unlikely happened and I really were diagnosed with cancer, what could I actually do about it?"

Coping Strategies: "As bad as a cancer diagnosis would be, it's unlikely that I would totally go to pieces. After an initial difficult adjustment to the fact—which might takes days to weeks—I would most likely begin to think about what I needed to do to deal with the situation. It would certainly be difficult, yet it wouldn't be a situation that I was less equipped to handle than anyone else. My doctor and I would plan the most effective possible treatment strategies. I would join a local cancer support group and get lots of support from my friends and immediate family. I would try alternative methods, such as visualization and dietary changes, which could help. In short, I would try everything possible to attempt to heal the condition."

Restructuring Unhelpful Self-Talk

Skill Building

The above three examples illustrate how overestimating thoughts can be challenged and then countered by more realistic, less anxiety-provoking thinking. During the next week, I would like you to monitor the times when you feel anxious or panicky. Each time you do, use the following five steps to work with negative self-talk. (These five steps are presented orally and are also included in the client manual.)

1. If you're feeling anxious or upset, do something to relax, such as abdominal breathing, progressive muscle relaxation, or meditation. It's easier to notice your internal dialogue when you take time to slow down and relax.

2. After you get somewhat relaxed, ask yourself, "What was I telling myself that made me anxious?" or "What was going through my mind?" Make an effort to separate thoughts from feelings. For example, "I felt terrified" describes a feeling, while "I will lose control of myself" is an overestimating thought which might lead you to feel terrified. Sometimes feelings and thoughts occur together in one statement: "I'm scared I will lose control!" The negative thought here is still "I will lose control."

3. Identify the two basic types of distortions within your anxious self-talk. Sort out *overestimating thoughts,* and *thoughts that underestimate your ability to cope.* Note that overestimating thoughts frequently begin with "What if . . ." Thoughts that underestimate your ability to cope might begin with "I can't . . ." or "I won't be able . . ."

4. When you've identified your anxious, distorted thoughts, *challenge* them with appropriate questions.

   For overestimating thoughts: "What are the realistic odds that this feared outcome will actually happen? Has this outcome ever happened to me before?"

For thoughts underestimating your ability to cope: "What coping skills can I bring to bear to handle anxiety? If the worst outcome I fear *does* occur, what could I actually *do* to cope?"

5. Write counterstatements to each of your overestimating thoughts. These counterstatements should contain language and logic that reflect more balanced, realistic thinking. Then make a list of ways you might cope with your phobic situation, including what you would do if your most feared outcome actually occurred.

Use the Worry Worksheet (next page) to write down your anxious thoughts and corresponding counterstatements for your specific fear or phobia. In the section at the bottom, list ways in which you would cope if the negative (but unlikely) outcome you fear actually occurred.

(Note: It is important to have the client identify and work through negative self-talk and counterstatements with respect to his or her specific phobia *in session.* Have the client fill out a copy of the Worry Worksheet and then give them extra copies to fill out at home.)

Summary of Session

(as in session 2)

Feedback From Client

(as in session 2)

Homework

Homework given for session 3 is as follows:

1. Use the Worry Worksheet (the client should receive ten copies) each day to work with anticipatory anxiety that comes up around facing your phobic situation. Write down overestimating "What if . . ." thoughts that keep the fear going, and refute each one with a more reasonable, self-supporting counterstatement. Then write down coping strategies, including both: 1) how you see yourself coping when you actually begin to confront your phobia, and 2) how you would cope if your worst fear about the situation came true. Bring in your worksheets to therapy the following week.

2. Continue practicing abdominal breathing and progressive muscle relaxation daily, as in the homework for session 2.

The Worry Worksheet

Specific Fear or Phobia _____

Anxious Self-Talk	Counterstatements
Overestimating thoughts (or images):	
"What if . . ."	

Coping Strategies: First, list ways in which you can cope with your phobic situation. Second, list ways in which you would cope if a negative (but unlikely) outcome did occur. Use the other side of the sheet if needed. Change "What if" to *"What I would do if* (one of your negative predictions actually did come about). . . ."

1.

2.

3.

Make twenty copies of this worksheet before you start, and use a separate sheet each time you practice disputing your negative self-talk.

Session 3—Main Points

- Explain the role of self-talk in perpetuating phobias.

- Have the client practice identifying the two types of distorted thinking that contribute to their particular phobia, i.e.,
    1. thoughts which overestimate a negative outcome, and
    2. thoughts which underestimate their ability to cope.

- Work with the client to challenge their erroneous self-statements and develop appropriate counterstatements.

- Encourage the client to continue using the Worry Worksheet at home on a daily basis.

- Assign homework.

Session 4

Anxiety Management Strategies

Monitoring of Current Status

(as in session 2)

Agenda

The purpose of this session is to teach the client strategies for handling panic should it occur when confronting their phobic situation, as well as methods for reducing worry (anticipatory anxiety) that is likely to occur in advance of undertaking exposure. Panic management strategies are usually addressed first. (It is preferable to refer to them as "anxiety management strategies" so as not to create an expectation of panic for the client.) It's particularly important for the client to learn panic management strategies if they have a history of panicking when confronting their phobic situation.

Worksheets for this session include The Anxiety Scale, Coping Statements, and Worry Reduction Techniques, and can be found in the client manual.

Review of Homework

Ask the client how their daily practice with the Worry Worksheet went. Common problems include:

1. **The client was not sufficiently relaxed to discern their own negative self-talk:** Reiterate that identifying and disputing self-talk is best done *after* episodes of being highly anxious or worried—i.e., when one is settled down. It is difficult to analyze one's inner dialogue in a state of acute, high anxiety.

2. **The client has difficulty countering negative self-talk:** Negative self-statements may not at first be sufficiently concrete and specific. It may be difficult to counter highly general statements such as "What if I lose control (come 'unglued,' go 'crazy,' etc.)?" During the session, have the client address general statements with the question "What would actually happen if . . . (the negative outcome occurred)?" Draw out their response until they specify in *detail* their negative scenarios about what might happen.

3. **The client is reluctant to disbelieve their own overestimations of danger or underestimations of their ability to cope:** This generally requires in-session assistance from the therapist. Engage the client in a dialogue in which you ask them about what specific evidence they have for their overestimating belief. An example follows:

Client: What if I had a heart attack from panicking while driving on the freeway?

Therapist: What is the evidence that panic attacks cause heart attacks?

Client: I don't know.

Therapist: In my experience, I've never heard of a panic attack causing a heart attack. There's simply no evidence for any relationship between cardiovascular disease and panic. Now, what would be a good counterstatement to your original "What if" statement?

Client: A panic attack, however uncomfortable, is not dangerous to my heart. I can let panic rise, fall, and pass, and my heart will still be fine.

If the client has difficulty believing they could cope, it is okay to suggest possible coping strategies (although it's always ideal if they can be encouraged to come up with their own). The following dialogue elicits the client's coping response:

Client: What if I'm home alone and start to panic? That would be *terrible*— I don't think I could handle it.

Therapist: Is it really true that panicking alone at home would be utterly terrible? What's the absolute worst that could happen? Would you actually die?

Client: No, of course I wouldn't die. I'd just be very frightened.

Therapist: Is it absolutely true that there is nothing you could do? That you'd be completely helpless, without recourse?

Client: No, I guess not. I would try and call John or else my friend, Cindy. If no one was available, I could call the local crisis hotline.

Concepts and Skills

The following concepts and skills should be taught to all clients, regardless of whether they have a history of panic attacks in the context of their phobia.

Psychoeducation

The Anxiety Scale

With practice you can learn to identify the preliminary signs that a panic attack may be imminent. For some individuals this might be a sudden quickening of heartbeat. For others it might be a tightening in the chest, sweaty hands, or queasiness. Still others might experience a slight dizziness or disorientation. Most people experience some preliminary warning symptoms before reaching the "point of no return" when a full-blown panic attack is inevitable.

It's possible to distinguish among different levels or degrees of anxiety by imagining a ten-point scale.

Anxiety Scale

7–10: *Major Panic Attack*	All of the symptoms in level 6 exaggerated; terror; fear of going crazy or dying; compulsion to escape
6: *Moderate Panic Attack*	Palpitations; difficulty breathing; feeling disoriented or detached (feeling of unreality); panic in response to perceived loss of control
5: *Early Panic*	Heart pounding or beating irregularly; constricted breathing; spaciness or dizziness; definite fear of losing control; compulsion to escape
4: *Marked Anxiety*	Feeling uncomfortable or "spacey"; heart beating fast; muscles tight; *beginning to question your ability to maintain control*
3: *Moderate Anxiety*	Feeling uncomfortable but still in control; heart starting to beat faster; more rapid breathing; muscles tightening; sweaty palms
2: *Mild Anxiety*	Butterflies in stomach; muscle tension; definitely nervous
1: *Slight Anxiety*	Passing twinge of anxiety, feeling slightly nervous
0: *Relaxation*	Calm, a feeling of being undistracted and at peace

The symptoms at various levels of this scale are typical, although they may not correspond exactly to your own symptoms. The important thing is to identify what constitutes a level 4 for *you*. This is the point at which——whatever symptoms you're experiencing—*you feel your control over your reaction beginning to diminish*. Up to and through level 3, you may be feeling anxious and uncomfortable, but you still feel that you're coping. Starting at level 4, you begin to wonder whether you can manage what's happening, which can lead you to escalate your anxiety further. With practice you can learn to "catch yourself" and limit your reaction *before* it reaches the point of no return. The more adept you become at recognizing slight to moderate levels of anxiety up through level 4 on the scale, the more control you will gain over your anxiety.

Abdominal Breathing

Abdominal breathing is the most important skill you can use to manage anxiety that comes up when facing a fearful situation. Three or four minutes of steady abdominal breathing will generally diminish mild to moderate levels of anxiety (levels 2 and 3 on the Anxiety Scale) and can usually interrupt the upward momentum of anxiety at level 4. Even if anxiety reaches a panic level, abdominal breathing can help to reduce it.

As a general rule, it's good to practice abdominal breathing just before you begin to confront your phobia and continue it the whole time you are in the situation. Focusing on your breathing will help to keep you more grounded, in the present, and less prone to focus on unconstructive thoughts.

Coping Statements

It's often helpful when confronting a phobia to work with coping statements. These are positive statements you can say to yourself just before you begin to face your phobic situation—or to help manage anxiety during the exposure process itself.

The purpose of using coping statements is to help divert your mind from any negative, anxiety-provoking self-talk you might be prone to engage in when you face what you fear. These positive statements also help put your mind in a positive frame. They can help you relax and maintain your confidence just before or during the time you confront your phobia. Any anxiety you experience during exposure to your phobia tends to make you more suggestible. By repeating positive coping statements at the time of exposure, you can suggest a positive state of mind that can help minimize anxiety.

There are two ways in which you might want to work with coping statements. First, you might want to record your favorite statements on an audio cassette and listen to them several times before you directly confront your phobic situation. If you have a portable cassette recorder with headphones, you might even want to listen to them during the exposure process itself.

An alternative, more active way to work with coping statements is to write them down on three-by-five file cards—one or two statements per card. Keep the cards in your purse or wallet and then take them out and rehearse the coping statements before or during your exposure sessions. Some people find repeating a single coping statement over and over to be more effective, while others like to read down a list of several coping statements.

Keep in mind that to get the most benefit from coping statements, you will need to practice working with them many times. They may not be as effective in off-setting anxiety the first few times you use them as they will be after repeated practice. It took many repetitions to reinforce your negative, anxiety-provoking self-statements that trigger your anxiety. By the same token, it will take repeated use of positive coping statements—before or during real-life exposure—to reach a point where you fully internalize them.

The following coping statements are divided into three categories: statements to use when you are preparing to face your phobic situation; statements you can use when you first confront the situation and during the exposure process; and, finally, statements you can use to help you handle any symptoms or feelings that come up during exposure.

Preparing to Face Your Phobia

- Today I'm willing to go just a little outside my comfort zone.

- This is an opportunity for me to learn to become comfortable with this situation.

- Facing my fear of _____ is the best way to overcome my anxiety about it.

- Each time I choose to face _____, I take another step toward becoming free of fear.

- By taking this step now, I'll eventually be able to do what I want.

- There's no right way to do this. Whatever happens is fine.

- I know I'll feel better once I'm actually in the situation.

- Whatever I do, I'll do the best I can.

- I praise myself for being willing to confront my fear of _____.

- There's always a way to retreat from this situation if I need to.

First Confronting (and During Exposure to) Your Phobia

- I've handled this before and I can handle it now.

- Relax and go slowly. There's no need to push right now.

- I can take some abdominal breaths and take my time.

- Nothing serious is going to happen to me.

- It's okay to take my time with this and do only as much as I'm ready to do today.

- I'm going to be all right. I've succeeded with this before.

- I don't have to do this perfectly. I can let myself be human.

- I can think about being in my peaceful place as I undertake this.

- I can monitor my anxiety level and retreat from this situation if I need to.

- This is not as bad as I thought.

- As I continue to practice exposure, it will get easier.

- If I'm feeling anxiety, I'm already in the process of desensitizing.

Coping With Body Sensations and Feelings That Come Up During Exposure

- I can handle these symptoms or sensations.

- These feelings are just a reminder to use my coping skills.

- I can take some abdominal breaths and allow these feelings to pass.

- These feelings will pass and I'll be okay.

- This is just adrenaline—it will pass in a few minutes.

- This will pass soon.

- These are just thoughts—not reality.

- This is just anxiety—I'm not going to let it get to me.

- Nothing about these sensations or feelings is dangerous.

- I don't need to let these feelings and sensations stop me. I can continue to function.

- It's always okay to retreat for a while if I need to.

- This feeling isn't comfortable or pleasant, but I can accept it.

- I'll just let my body do its thing. This will pass.

- I can take all the time I need in order to let go and relax.

- There's no need to push myself. I can take as small a step forward as I choose.

- This anxiety won't hurt me—even if it doesn't feel good.

- I don't need these thoughts—I can choose to think differently.

Other Diversion Techniques

Any technique that helps you to redirect your attention away from anxiety symptoms and fear-provoking thoughts can be helpful when you're confronting your phobic situation. While abdominal breathing and coping statements should be your first line of defense, any of the following strategies can be useful, especially at levels of anxiety up to and including level 4 in the Anxiety Scale.

- Talk to another person (this could be your support person or someone you call on a cellular phone).

- Move around or engage in physical activity.

- Engage in a simple, repetitive activity (count from 100 backwards during a long elevator ride, for example).

- Express angry feelings (get angry at the phobia—but do *not* vent anger on people).

- Anchor yourself in your immediate environment. Focus on concrete objects in your surroundings, even touch them if that helps.

- Practice thought stopping. Shout the word "stop" once or twice—or snap a rubber band against your wrist. This will help disrupt a chain of negative thoughts. Follow this with abdominal breathing or by repeating a positive affirmation.

Putting It All Together: Integrated Anxiety Management

In general, should anxiety symptoms come on during exposure, use the following three-step technique to manage them. (Some clients may want to think of this as the "ABC technique" to help remember the steps.)

Accept the symptoms. Don't fight or resist them. Resisting or fleeing symptoms of anxiety tends to make them worse. The more you can adopt an attitude of acceptance, no matter how unpleasant the symptoms may be, the better your ability to cope. Acceptance prepares you to do something proactive about your anxiety rather than getting caught up in reactions to it.

(The books by Claire Weekes, *Hope and Help For Your Nerves* (1978), and *Peace From Nervous Suffering* (1978), can be a useful adjunct in helping clients to understand the attitude of acceptance.)

Breathe. Practice abdominal breathing. When anxiety first comes up, always go to abdominal breathing. If you have been practicing abdominal breathing regularly, merely initiating it provides a cue to your body to relax and disengage from a potential "fight or flight" response.

Cope. Use a coping strategy. After you begin to feel centered in abdominal breathing, use a coping statement or a diversion technique (for example, talking to your support person) to continue to manage your feelings during exposure. *Any* coping technique will reinforce the basic stance of not giving attention or energy to negative thoughts and/or uncomfortable body sensations. By regularly practicing coping techniques, you reinforce an attitude of efficacy and mastery—instead of passive submission and victimization—in the face of your anxiety. Be aware that abdominal breathing is itself a coping strategy, and sometimes it alone will be enough.

What to Do If Anxiety Exceeds Level 4

If you are unable to arrest an anxiety reaction before it goes beyond your personal "point of no return," observe the following guidelines:

- Leave the situation if possible. Try to return to it later the same day if you can.

- Don't try to control or fight your symptoms—accept them and "ride them out"; remind yourself that your reaction is not dangerous and will pass.

- Talk to someone, if available. Express your feelings to them (if in a car or aboard a plane alone, you might use a cellular phone).

- Move around or engage in physical activity.

- Focus on simple objects around you.

- Touch the floor, the physical objects around you, or "ground" yourself in some other way.

- Breathe slowly and regularly through your nose to reduce possible symptoms of hyperventilation.

- As a last resort, take an extra dose of a minor tranquilizer (with the approval of your doctor).

If you have a panic attack, you may feel temporarily very confused and disorientated. Try asking yourself the following questions to increase your objectivity (you may want to write these out on a three-by-five card that you carry with you during exposure).

1. *Are these symptoms I'm feeling truly dangerous?* (Answer: No)

2. *What is the absolute worst thing that could happen?* (Usual answer: I might have to leave this situation quickly or I might have to ask for assistance.)

3. *Am I telling myself anything that is making this worse?*

4. *What is the most supportive thing I could do for myself right now?*

(The following reeducation about panic attacks is reserved for clients who have a substantial fear of panic during exposure—something less common with specific phobias but occasionally seen. It is unnecessary to offer these explanations to a majority of clients with specific phobia—only those for whom fear of panic is particularly salient.)

Understanding and Managing Panic Attacks

The Panic Cycle. A panic attack is a surge of mounting physiological arousal that can occur in response to encountering—or merely thinking about—a phobic situation. Physical symptoms include heart palpitations, tightening in the chest, shortness of breath, dizziness, faintness, sweating, nausea, trembling, shaking, or tingling in the hands and feet. Psychological reactions that accompany these bodily changes include an intense desire to run away, feelings of unreality, and fears of having a heart attack, going crazy, or doing something uncontrollable.

The panic cycle involves an interaction between bodily symptoms of anxiety and fearful thoughts. The cycle looks like this:

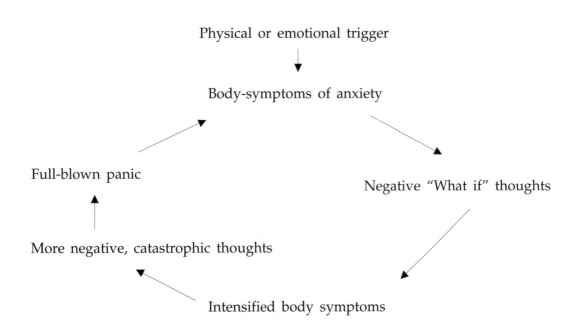

Hyperventilation may, in some cases, contribute to the loop. Rapid, shallow breathing during early stages of panic may produce hyperventilation symptoms such as tingling in the hands and feet, dizziness, confusion, and feelings of unreality. Be aware, however, that panic attacks can produce these symptoms in the absence of hyperventilation.

The following concepts are very useful for learning to cope with panic attacks:

Panic Attacks Are Not Dangerous. Recognize that a panic attack is nothing more than the well-known fight-or-flight response occurring out of context. This is a natural bodily response that enables you (and all other mammals) to be alerted to and quickly flee a truly life-threatening situation. What makes a panic attack hard to cope with is that this intense reaction occurs in a situation that poses no obvious or life-threatening danger, such as seeing a spider, riding an elevator, or receiving a shot. Because there is no realistic, external danger, *your mind tends to invent or attribute danger* to the intense bodily symptoms you're going through. Your mind can very quickly go through the process: "If I feel this bad, I must be in some danger."

In short, you may imagine that heart palpitations will lead to a heart attack, that your constricted breathing will lead to suffocation, that dizzy sensations will result in fainting, or that you will lose control and "go crazy." In fact, none of these ever occurs. You can't have a heart attack from a panic attack. Your heart is made of very strong and dense muscle fibers. According to Dr. Claire Weekes, a noted authority on panic, a healthy heart can beat 200 beats per minute for days—even weeks—without sustaining any damage. Electrocardiogram tracings of panic attacks show rapid heartbeat, but none of the types of abnormalities seen in individuals with heart conditions. By the same token, you can't suffocate from a panic attack. Your brain has a built-in reflex mechanism that will *force* you to breathe if you're not getting enough oxygen. Feelings of faintness or dizziness may come on because of reduced circulation to the brain during panic, but you won't faint. These sensations can be relieved by slow, abdominal breathing. It's also important to know that if you panic you will *never* lose control or "act crazy." It's unheard of. At worst, you will simply withdraw from the situation.

The upshot of all this is that *a panic attack is not dangerous.* If you can convince yourself of this at the time panic occurs, you may significantly reduce the intensity of your reaction.

Don't Fight Panic. It's important to avoid fighting a panic attack—for example, tensing up against panic symptoms or trying to force them to go away. This only increases muscle tension, which is one of the contributing causes of panic. In her books, *Hope and Help for Your Nerves* and *Peace From Nervous Suffering*, Claire Weekes describes a four-step process that many people have found very helpful:

1. Face panic symptoms rather than running from them. Instead of telling yourself, "I can't handle this," you might say, "This will pass . . . I've handled it before and I'll manage it this time, too."

2. Accept what your body is going through. Again, don't fight panic. Work on adopting an attitude of acceptance. Ideally, *learn to observe* your body's state of physiological arousal, no matter how uncomfortable it may be, instead of reacting to it. *Acceptance of the symptoms of panic is the most important attitude you can bring to bear in increasing your ability to cope.*

3. Be willing to float with the "wave" of a panic attack, instead of forcing your way through it. You might imagine that you are literally riding a wave, moving with the upsurge and gradual fading out of panic. Realize that it takes only a few minutes for most of the adrenaline produced by panic to be reabsorbed, so that the worst will be over quickly.

4. Allow time to pass. Realize that reactions you're going through are time-limited. Say to yourself, "This will pass," and engage in some distracting activity, such as conversation, moving around, abdominal breathing, or repeating positive statements until the reaction subsides.

Worry (Anticipatory Anxiety) Management Strategies

Ultimately the best treatment for anticipatory anxiety—worry in advance of facing a phobia—is exposure. Anticipatory anxiety may not clear up entirely until you have mastered your phobic situation. You can count on being relatively free of worry about your phobia when you've desensitized to it and no longer have the need to avoid it.

Prior to undertaking exposure, you are likely to have some worry about facing your fear, if you don't worry about it already. Worry is like a negative spiral. The longer you spend time with it, the deeper into it you can get. It may also be viewed as a form of trance. The more you induce it by repetition, the more entranced you may become, and the more difficult it is to "break the spell."

It takes a deliberate act of will to stop worry. You need to make a deliberate effort to move away from circular mental activity in your mind by "shifting gears" to another modality of experience, such as bodily activity, expressing emotions, interpersonal communication, sensory distraction, or a specific ritual. Although deliberately choosing to break out of an obsessive worry may be difficult at first (especially if you're highly anxious), with practice it will get easier.

Here are a few strategies that will help you to move away from worry.

Do physical exercise. This can be your favorite outdoor or indoor exercise, dancing, or just household chores. Focus on your body while doing the exercise.

Do progressive muscle relaxation alone or in combination with abdominal breathing. Keep this up for five to twenty minutes until you feel relaxed and free of worry-thoughts.

Take action on the issue that causes you worry. If you're afraid of flying, read a book or listen to tape on overcoming that fear (see Resources—appendix 3). If you're afraid of getting a shot, practice your imagery desensitization. If you're afraid of contracting cancer, devote energy to health practices such as exercise and good nutrition.

Talk to someone. Converse (in person or on the phone) about something other than the worry, unless you want to express your feelings about it.

Confront your worry on paper. Write out on a piece of paper the negative "What if" statements that make up your worry. Then take another sheet and write constructive counterstatements to each of your What if statements (use the Worry Worksheet from the previous week, if you wish).

Use visual distractions. This can be TV, movies, video games, your computer, uplifting reading, or even a rock garden.

Use sensory-motor distraction. Try arts and crafts, repairing something, gardening.

Practice healthy rituals. Combine abdominal breathing with a positive affirmation that has personal significance. Keep this up for five to ten minutes, or until you're fully relaxed. (This is actually a positive trance induction to overcome the negative trance enforced by the obsessive worry.)

Examples of affirmations: *(for the spiritually inclined)*

- "Let it go."   - "Let go and let God."

- "These are just thoughts—   - "I Abide in Spirit (God)."
  they're fading away."

- "I'm whole, relaxed, and free of   - "I release this negativity to God."
  worry."

Use thought stopping. Say the word "Stop!" emphatically several times. If you prefer, snap a rubber band against your wrist or throw a wet washrag over your face. Following this, use any of the preceding techniques. Thought stopping alone will probably only temporarily disrupt a worry pattern, but it is a good way to initially break that pattern.

Remember that you can stop worrying by using any or all of these strategies. *It is necessary, however, to practice.* The more you utilize these techniques, the more mastery you will achieve in overcoming useless worry.

(It is important to discuss these strategies with the client in session. Ask them which ones they would be willing to try. Then give them homework to practice these specific techniques at home during the week when worry arises.)

Summary of Session

(as in session 2)

Feedback from Client

(as in session 2)

Homework

Homework for this week is as follows:

1. Practice anxiety-management techniques, including abdominal breathing, coping statements, and diversion techniques at any time when you feel anxiety symptoms coming on during the week. After you have become proficient at using several different techniques, try combining coping statements or diversion techniques with abdominal breathing. Remember the three-step strategy: *accept* anxiety symptoms, *breathe* slowly from your abdomen to reduce them, then *cope*, applying coping statements or other diversion techniques until you feel better. Remember that sometimes abdominal breathing alone for a few minutes will be all you need to do.

2. Use worry mangement techniques to directly offset the tendency to worry whenever it arises during the week. Pick two or three preferred techniques from the list and practice them regularly.

3. Continue challenging and restructuring negative self-talk associated with your phobia using the Worry Worksheet.

4. Continue practicing abdominal breathing and progressive muscle relaxation on a regular basis.

Session 4—Main Points

- Teach the client to use the Anxiety Scale. Be sure they know how to identify what constitutes level 4 *for them*.

- Teach the client about abdominal breathing (which they have been practicing for two weeks) as a powerful technique for limiting anxiety during exposure.

- Explain the usefulness of coping statements and have the client identify (from the list) those they would prefer to use when facing their phobia.

- Go over the list of "other diversion techniques," asking the client about any they've used in the past as well as those they'd consider using when they face their phobia.

- Review the guidelines for how to manage anxiety when it exceeds level 4.

- Provide education about how to cope with panic attacks for those clients who are specifically fearful of panic during exposure.

- If time permits, review the list of worry management techniques intended to help the client cope with anticipatory anxiety.

- Homework Assignments.

Session 5

Imagery Desensitization

Monitoring of Current Status

(as in session 2)

Agenda

This session is devoted entirely to teaching the client imagery desensitization. It involves setting up a stimulus hierarchy for the client's specific phobia and having them actually visualize and relax to the first scene or two of that hierarchy. Although imagery desensitization is not done by some therapists, I feel it helps the client to achieve some desensitization before undertaking real-life exposure. Imagery desensitization is the *only* intervention possible (unless the therapist has access to video tapes or virtual exposure) when the phobic situation cannot be simulated in real life—e.g., a phobia of earthquakes or tornadoes.

Review of Homework

Ask the client how they did with implementing anxiety and worry-management techniques to offset episodes of anticipatory anxiety. Reiterate that anxiety-management techniques are especially helpful when levels of somatic anxiety are high, while worry management techniques can be used to divert attention away from useless, perseverating thoughts (worry).

The most common problem that arises is that the client lacks confidence that the techniques can actually work. They may have tried them once or twice, with limited or no results, and then given up. It's important to emphasize that these coping techniques require considerable rehearsal to become effective. It will be necessary, for example, to practice coping statements many times before they become effective in diverting attention away from anxiety as well as reframing the client's attitude when anxiety arises. A learning curve is always involved in gaining proficiency with these techniques.

A separate but related issue is that the client hasn't learned to discriminate the earliest cues or warning signs of incipient anxiety. Work with them until they are clear on how *they* define *their own* levels 1, 2, 3, and 4 on the Anxiety Scale. As they gain skill in catching anxiety episodes at the earliest possible stage, the coping techniques will tend to work better.

This is a good time to introduce self-monitoring, which is otherwise not an essential feature of this treatment protocol. Have the client keep a daily record during the week of specific episodes of anxiety or worry, rating the intensity of these episodes before and after utilizing a coping technique. They can then bring in their records for discussion the following week.

Concepts and Skills

Psychoeducation

The most effective way to overcome a phobia is simply to face it. Continuing to avoid a situation that frightens you is, more than anything else, what keeps the phobia alive.

Having to face a particular situation you have been avoiding for years may at the outset seem an impossible task. Yet this task can be made manageable by breaking it down into a number of small steps. Instead of entering a situation all at once, you can do it very gradually in small or even minute increments. And instead of confronting the situation directly in real life, you can face it first in your imagination. This is where imagery desensitization comes in.

Sensitization is a process of becoming sensitized to a particular stimulus. In the case of phobias, it involves learning to associate anxiety with a particular situation. Perhaps you once panicked or experienced high anxiety while confronting your phobic situation. If your anxiety level was high enough, it's likely that you acquired a strong association between being in that particular situation and being anxious. Thereafter, being in, near, or perhaps just thinking about the situation automatically triggered your anxiety: a connection between the situation and a strong anxiety response was established. Because this connection was automatic and seemingly beyond your control, you probably did all you could to avoid putting yourself in the situation again. Your avoidance was rewarded because it saved you from reexperiencing your anxiety. At the point where you began to *always* avoid the situation, you developed a full-fledged phobia.

Desensitization is the process of *unlearning* the connection between anxiety and a particular situation. For desensitization to occur, you need to enter your phobic situation while you're in a relaxed state. With *imagery desensitization,* you *visualize* being in a phobic situation while you're relaxed. If you begin to feel anxious, you retreat from your imagined phobic situation and imagine yourself instead in a very peaceful scene. With *real-life desensitization,* you confront a phobic situation directly but physically retreat to a safe place if your anxiety reaches a certain level—then return to the situation. In both cases the point is to 1) *unlearn* the connection between a phobic situation (such as getting a shot or riding an elevator) and an anxiety response, and 2) *reassociate* feelings of relaxation and calmness with that particular situation. Repeatedly visualizing a phobic situation while relaxed—or actually entering it while relaxed—will eventually allow you to overcome your tendency to respond with anxiety. If you can train yourself to relax in response to something, you will no longer feel anxious about it. Relaxation and anxiety are incompatible responses, so the goal of desensitization is to learn to remain in the phobic situation and be relaxed at the same time.

You may wonder why it's necessary to go through the desensitization process initially in your imagination. Why not just face the dreaded object or situation in real life? More than thirty years ago, the behavioral psychologist Joseph Wolpe discovered the efficacy of desensitization through imagery. In some cases it is so effective that it supplants the need for real-life desensitization. In other cases, imagery desensitization reduces anxiety sufficiently to make the task of real-life desensitization easier.

Practicing imagery desensitization before confronting a phobia in real life can also help you overcome your anticipatory anxiety. As you learned in the previous session, this is the anxiety you experience in anticipation of having to deal with a phobic situation. Hours or days before riding an elevator or your next flight, for example, you may experience numerous anxious thoughts and images about the upcoming situation. Dwelling on these anxious thoughts and images only creates more anxiety, long before you ever deal with the actual situation. By systematically training yourself to relax as you imagine scenes of a future phobic situation, you can reduce your anticipatory anxiety substantially.

Success with imagery desensitization depends on four things:

1. Your capacity to attain a deep state of relaxation.

2. Constructing an appropriate *hierarchy*: a series of scenes or situations relating to your phobia which are ranked from mildly anxiety-provoking to very anxiety-provoking.

3. The vividness and detail with which you can visualize each scene in the hierarchy.

4. Your patience and perseverance in practicing desensitization on a regular basis.

A hierarchy is helpful because each new step is only slightly more anxiety-provoking than the one before, so you can progress very gradually toward a full confrontation with your fear.

Skill Building

Constructing an Appropriate Hierarchy

A well-constructed hierarchy allows you to approach a phobic situation gradually through a sequence of steps. The following steps are involved:

1. Select the phobic situation you want to work on.

2. Imagine having to deal with this situation in a very limited way—one that hardly bothers you at all. You can create this scenario by imagining yourself somewhat removed in space or time from full exposure to the situation—such as merely walking up to an elevator without going in, or imagining your feelings one month before you are going to make a flight. Or you can diminish the difficulty of the situation by visualizing yourself with a supportive person at your side. Try in these ways to create a very mild scenario of facing your phobia and designate it as the first step in your hierarchy.

3. Now imagine what would be the strongest or most challenging scene relating to your phobia, and place it at the opposite extreme as the highest step in your hierarchy. For example, if you're phobic about supermarkets, your highest step might be waiting in a long, busy line at the checkout counter by yourself. For flying, such a step might involve taking off on a transcontinental flight or encountering severe air turbulence midflight.

4. Now develop six to eight scenes of varying intensity between your mildest and most challenging scene. Place these scenes in ascending order between the two extremes you've already defined. See if you can identify what specific parameters of your phobia make you more or less anxious and use them to develop scenes of varying intensity.

There are four different variables you might consider in developing imagery scenes of varying intensity:

Spatial proximity. How close you are physically to the feared object or situation. In the case of flying, for example, you would likely feel more anxiety watching planes land and take off than you would merely seeing the airport terminal. Or seeing a picture of a jet might be less anxiety-provoking than standing next to one in real life.

Temporal proximity. How close you are in time to the feared object or situation. For example, you might be likely to feel more anxiety one hour before receiving a shot or taking an exam than the night before or three days before.

Length or duration of exposure. This refers to how long you are in a situation. Ten minutes in a shopping mall is likely to be more difficult than two minutes.

Intensity of exposure. Intensity of exposure is often closely related to duration. Riding up twenty floors in an elevator is a stronger, more intense exposure than riding up five floors. Having a blood sample taken is usually a more intense exposure than getting a shot, which is in turn more intense than watching someone else receive a shot.

Degree of support. How close you are to a support person during exposure. In driving on a freeway, you might imagine your support person sitting next to you, following you in a second car, following you a half mile back, or simply waiting for you at your destination.

Your hierarchy may vary in terms of just one of these variables or perhaps three or four. For example, the following hierarchy relating to driving on freeways varies in terms of three distinct parameters: 1) duration (or distance) driven, 2) degree of support, 3) degree of traffic congestion (one aspect of intensity).

Phobia About Driving on Freeways

1. Watching from a distance as cars drive past on the freeway

2. Riding in a car on the freeway with someone else driving (this could be broken down into several steps, varying the distance traveled or time spent on the freeway)

3. Driving on the freeway the distance of one exit with a support person sitting next to you at a time when there is little traffic

4. Driving the distance of one exit with a support person when the freeway is busier (but not at rush hour)

5. Repeat step 3 alone

6. Repeat step 4 alone

7. Driving the distance of two or three exits with a support person sitting next to you at a time when there is little traffic

8. Driving the distance of two or three exits with a support person sitting next to you at a time when there is moderate traffic

9. Repeat step 7 alone

10. Repeat step 8 alone

In steps above this level you would increase the distance you drive and also include driving under rush hour conditions.

In the next example (involving getting a shot), the hierarchy varies in terms of spatial proximity and intensity of exposure.

Phobia About Getting Injections

1. Watching a movie in which a minor character gets a shot

2. A friend talking about her flu shot

3. Making a routine doctor's appointment

4. Driving to a medical center

5. Parking your car in the medical center parking lot

6. Thinking about shots in the doctor's waiting room

7. A woman coming out of the treatment room rubbing her arm

8. A nurse with a tray of syringes walking past

9. Entering an examination room

10. A doctor entering the room and asking you about your symptoms

11. The doctor saying you need an injection

12. A nurse entering the room with injection materials

13. The nurse filling a syringe

14. The smell of alcohol being applied to a cotton ball

15. A hypodermic needle poised in the doctor's hand

16. Receiving a penicillin shot in the buttocks

17. Receiving a flu shot in the arm

18. Having a large blood sample taken

Note that in both examples, increments from one step to the next are very small. One of the keys to success with imagery desensitization is to create a hierarchy with small enough steps so that it's relatively easy to progress from one to the next.

Generally, eight to twelve steps in a hierarchy are sufficient, although in some cases you may want to include as many as twenty. Fewer than eight steps is usually an insufficient number to make the hierarchy meaningful.

Procedure for Imagery Desensitization

Desensitization through imagery is a two-step process. First, you need to take the time to get very relaxed. Second, you go through the desensitization process itself, which involves alternating back and forth between visualizing a particular scene in your hierarchy and recapturing a feeling of deep relaxation. Be sure to follow all of the steps outlined below:

1. *Relax.* Spend ten to fifteen minutes getting relaxed. Use progressive muscle relaxation or any other relaxation technique that works well for you.

2. *Visualize yourself in your peaceful scene.* This is the relaxing place you have been visualizing when you practice relaxation.

3. *Visualize yourself in the first scene of your phobia hierarchy.* Stay there for one minute, trying to picture everything with as much vividness and detail as possible, as if you were "right there." Do *not* picture yourself as being anxious. If you see yourself in the scene at all, imagine yourself acting and feeling calm and confident—dealing with the situation in the way you would most like to. If you feel little or no anxiety (below level 2 on the Anxiety Scale), proceed to the next scene up in your hierarchy.

4. *If you experience mild to moderate anxiety (level 2 or 3 on the Anxiety Scale), spend one minute in the scene, allowing yourself to relax to it.* You can do this by breathing away any anxious sensations in your body or by repeating coping statements from the list you received last week, such as "I am calm and at ease," or "Let go and relax." Picture yourself handling the situation in a calm and confident manner.

5. *After one minute of exposure to the scene, retreat from the phobic scene to your peaceful scene.* Spend about one minute in your peaceful scene or long enough to get fully relaxed. Then repeat your visualization of the same phobic scene as in step 4 for one minute. Keep alternating between a given phobic scene and your peaceful scene (about one minute each) until the phobic scene loses its capacity to elicit any (or more than very mild) anxiety. Remember to use abdominal breathing and coping statements to diminish any anxiety you feel. Then you are ready to proceed to the next step up in your hierarchy.

6. *If visualizing a particular scene causes you marked anxiety (level 4 or above on the Anxiety Scale), do not spend more than ten seconds there.* Retreat immediately to your peaceful scene and stay there until you're fully relaxed. If you have difficulty relaxing in your peaceful scene, do progressive muscle relaxation for five to ten minutes until you get relaxed. Expose yourself gradually to the more difficult scenes, alternating short intervals of exposure with retreat to your peaceful scene. If a particular scene in your hierarchy continues to cause difficulty, you probably need to add another step—one that is intermediate in difficulty between the last step you completed successfully and the one that is troublesome.

7. *Continue progressing up your hierarchy step by step in imagination.* Generally it will take a minimum of two exposures to an anxiety-provoking scene to reduce your anxiety to it. An exception might be when you're desensitizing to the first few scenes in your hierarchy. Keep in mind that it's important not to proceed to a more advanced step until you're fully comfortable with the preceding step. Practice imagery desensitization for fifteen to twenty minutes each day and begin your practice *not* with a new step but with the last step you successfully negotiated (then proceed to a new step).

To sum up, imagery desensitization involves four steps that you apply to *each* scene in your hierarchy:

1. *Visualize* the phobic scene as vividly and in as much detail as possible.

2. *React to the scene* allowing yourself to stay with it for one minute if your anxiety stays below level 4—marked anxiety. Picture yourself handling the scene in a calm and confident manner. Use abdominal breathing and coping statements to assist you in relaxing to the scene. If your anxiety to the scene reaches level 4 or above, retreat to your peaceful scene after five to ten seconds of exposure. If you still feel anxious in your peaceful scene, do ten to fifteen minutes of progressive muscle relaxation until you feel relaxed.

3. *Relax* in your peaceful scene (between exposures to phobic scenes) for up to a minute, until you're fully calm.

4. *Repeat* the process of alternating between a phobic scene and your peaceful scene until the phobic scene loses its power to elicit anxiety. At this point proceed to the next scene up in your hierarchy.

Getting the Most Out of Imagery Desensitization

The process of desensitization will work best if you adhere to the following guidelines:

❖

Spend about fifteen to twenty minutes the first time you practice imagery desensitization. As you gain skill in relaxation and visualization, you can lengthen your sessions to thirty minutes. In this time period (on a good day), you can expect to master two or three scenes in your hierarchy.

❖

You need to be very relaxed for imagery desensitization to be effective. If you feel that you aren't deeply relaxed, then you might spend more time—twenty to thirty minutes—relaxing at the outset, and also spend more time relaxing in your peaceful scene after each exposure to a particular phobic scene. Make sure that you *fully* recover from any anxiety after each exposure.

❖

You need to be able to visualize each phobic scene as well as your peaceful scene in detail, as if you were actually there. If you have difficulty with visualizing effectively, you might ask yourself the following questions about each scene to heighten its vividness and detail:

- What objects or people are in the scene?

- What colors do you see in the scene?

- Is the light bright or dim?

- What sounds can you hear in the scene?

- Can you hear the wind or a breeze?

- What is the temperature of the air?

- What are you wearing?

- Can you smell or taste anything?

- What other physical sensations are you aware of?

- What are your emotions within the scene?

❖

Stop a particular session if you feel tired, bored, or overly upset.

❖

Try to practice every day if possible. Your general anxiety level may vary from day to day, so practicing every day for two weeks will give you the opportunity to desensitize under various conditions.

❖

Even if the first few scenes in your hierarchy don't elicit any anxiety at all, it's important to expose yourself to each of them at least once. (You can proceed from one to the next without retreating to your peaceful scene if your anxiety stays below level 2.) Imagery desensitization is at work even when you're not feeling any anxiety in response to a given scene because you are still associating relaxation with your phobia.

❖

Keep practicing until you have completed all of the scenes in your hierarchy.

Note: At this point the therapist should conduct imagery desensitization in session to the first two or three scenes of the client's hierarchy. The most tricky aspect of doing imagery is that the client may tend to avoid entering into the phobic scene completely. To enhance their involvement with imagery, try asking the following questions:

- What are you feeling?

- What's going through your mind?

- What's happening now?

Repeating questions such as these periodically should help keep the client focused and involved in a given scene.]

Putting Imagery Desensitization on Tape

You might find it helpful to put instructions for desensitization on tape to reduce any distractions while going through the process. Use the guidelines below for making your own tape.

- Begin your tape with ten to fifteen minutes of instructions for deep relaxation. Use the instructions for progressive muscle relaxation or any visualization that can induce a state of deep relaxation.

- Following the relaxation phase, visualize yourself in your peaceful scene. Spend at least one minute there.

- After going to your peaceful scene, record your own instructions for desensitization, according to the guidelines below:

Picture yourself in the first scene of your phobia hierarchy. . . . Imagine what it would be like if you were actually there.

(Pause fifteen to twenty seconds.)

Now allow yourself to relax in this scene . . . do whatever you need to do to relax.

(Pause fifteen to twenty seconds.)

Picture yourself handling the situation in just the way you would like . . . . Imagine that you are feeling relaxed, calm, and confident. You might wish to practice slow, abdominal breathing . . . and as you exhale, let out any tense or uncomfortable feelings. Also use your coping statements to relax if you wish.

(Pause fifteen to twenty seconds.)

Now let go of this scene and go back to your peaceful scene. Remain there until you feel fully relaxed. Put your recorder on pause if you need to until all of your anxiety is gone.

(Let one minute elapse on the tape, then continue.)

If you felt any anxiety imagining the previous scene in your hierarchy, go back and imagine yourself there again. . . . Take one minute to let go and relax in the context of that scene, and then return to your peaceful scene until you are fully relaxed. . . . You can place your cassette player on pause while you do this. . . . If you felt little or no anxiety within the previous scene, you're ready to go on.

(Leave a ten-second pause on the tape, then continue.)

Now, if you were fully relaxed in the previous scene, go on to the next scene in your hierarchy. . . . Imagine what it would be like if you were actually there.

(Pause fifteen to twenty seconds.)

(Repeat the above instructions a second time, starting from the phrase: "Now allow yourself to relax in this scene . . .")

Your tape should consist of 1) ten to fifteen minutes of instructions for deep relaxation, 2) instructions for going to your peaceful scene, with a minute of silence for being there, and 3) the above instructions for systematic desensitization repeated twice.

(Audio tapes by the author containing imagery desensitization protocols are available for the following phobias: fear of flying, heights, driving freeways, driving far from home, shopping in a supermarket, fear of contracting illness, giving a talk, and speaking up in public. For further information, contact New Harbinger Publications at (800) 748-6273.)

Summary of Session

(as in session 2)

Feedback from Client

(as in session 2)

Homework

1. Practice imagery desensitization for your phobia three to five times during the week. Spend up to thirty minutes each time. Work up the steps of your hierarchy following the procedure you received. You may wish to put instructions for imagery desensitization on tape.

   Please note: If you're having difficulty reducing your anxiety with imagery desensitization, the problem may lie in one of four areas. You may need to:

   - Be more completely relaxed before you begin—desensitization works best when you're very relaxed.

   - Work on visualizing your phobic scenes, or your peaceful scene, in more detail.

   - Become completely desensitized to a particular step in your hierarchy before proceeding to the next step, or

   - Add additional steps in your hierarchy, especially if the gap between one scene and the next one up is too wide.

2. Practice anxiety and worry management skills from session 4 as needed.

3. Continue practicing abdominal breathing and progressive muscle relaxation daily.

Session 5—Main Points

- Explain the concepts of sensitization and desensitization.

- Explain the rationale for doing imagery desensitization prior to real-life desensitization.

- Have the client construct a hierarchy of scenes relevant to their phobia for imagery desensitization. Make sure they identify all of the variables that influence the relative intensity of the various scenes.

- Go over the procedure for imagery desensitization in detail.

- Have the client follow the procedure for imagery desensitization to the first scene or two of their hierarchy *in session*.

- If the client has difficulty visualizing, assist them to relax more deeply or ask questions to help them develop their scene(s) in more detail.

- Homework Assignments.

Explanation of Exposure

Monitoring of Current Status

(as in session 2)

Agenda

This is a most critical session where the concept, rationale, and methodology of exposure therapy is presented. I devote the entire sixth session to explaining the nature and process of exposure. In the following session, the therapist actually begins to conduct *in vivo* exposure with the client or trains a support person (in session) to do so.

Review of Homework

Ask the client how their home practice with imagery desensitization went. (They should have practiced, ideally, every day or a minimum of three times.) Common problems that may have occurred include:

1. *The client has no anxiety at any step of their hierarchy:* Deepen relaxation prior to practicing desensitization so it is easier to visualize hierarchy scenes in detail. (Have the client relax in session to see if they are following the steps of progressive muscle relaxation correctly. *Or* use an alternative relaxation technique.)

Improve visualization by using the list of questions included in session 5 under "Getting the Most Out of Imagery Desensitization." Have the client practice visualizing detailed scenes of their phobic situation in session.

Modify imagery in the phobic scenes to include *bodily triggers of anxiety* as part of the imagery. For example: "As the elevator doors close, you feel your heart start to pound and your palms grow sweaty." Make sure the added imagery corresponds to the client's most troublesome body symptoms.

2. *The client has too much anxiety to practice:* Deepen relaxation by spending more time with progressive muscle relaxation or using an alternate technique.

If anxiety occurs at the beginning of the hierarchy, add additional preliminary scenes of lower intensity.

If anxiety occurs in the middle or late in the hierarchy, add intermediate scenes.

Make sure the client is withdrawing from difficult scenes at the first sign that anxiety is reaching level 4 on the Anxiety Scale, and then staying in their peaceful scene until fully relaxed. Have them practice imagery desensitization in session, using finger signals to denote: 1) their anxiety levels and 2) when they retreat and return to a given phobic scene. It should be possible to fine tune the process of exposure and retreat from difficult scenes until the client is able to tolerate the scene at anxiety levels below level 4.

Concepts and Skills

Psychoeducation—Real-Life Desensitization (Exposure)

Real-life desensitization is the single most effective available treatment for phobias. While imagery desensitization is often an important prerequisite, actually facing the situations that you have been avoiding in real life is essential for recovery.

Other terms for real-life desensitization are *in vivo desensitization, exposure therapy,* or simply *exposure*. In many controlled studies, direct exposure to phobic situations has consistently been found to be more effective than other, nonbehavioral treatments such as insight therapy, cognitive therapy by itself, or medication. Nothing works better for overcoming a fear than facing it—especially when this is done systematically and in small increments. Improvement resulting from real-life exposure does not disappear weeks or months later. Once you've fully desensitized yourself to a phobic situation in real life, you can remain free of fear.

For all its effectiveness, exposure isn't always a particularly easy or comfortable process to go through. Not everyone is willing to tolerate the unpleasantness of facing phobic situations or to persist with practicing real-life desensitization on a regular basis. Exposure therapy demands a strong commitment on your part. If you're genuinely committed to your recovery, then you'll be willing to:

- Take the risk to face your phobic situation

- Tolerate the initial discomfort that entering your phobic situation—even in small increments—sometimes involves

- *Persist in practicing* exposure on a consistent basis, despite probable setbacks, over a long enough period of time to overcome your fear

If you're ready to make a genuine commitment to exposure, you will very likely recover from your phobia.

(**Note:** At this point it is useful to explore and discuss the client's level of commitment to undertaking exposure. If such commitment is shaky, offer reassurance that exposure is manageable through the use of incremental steps and a support person.)

The basic procedure for exposure is essentially the same as for imagery desensitization, with a few modifications, particularly involving your hierarchy of situations and the use of a support person.

Constructing an Exposure Hierarchy

You can use the same basic hierarchy of phobic scenes you constructed for your imagery desensitization. The difference is that you will be carrying out the steps of your hierarchy in real life rather than in your imagination. So you may find you need to add some additional steps to your real-life hierarchy to make transitions from step to step easier. You may need more (and smaller) steps when you face a situation in real life than when you're visualizing it in your mind.

If some of your imagery hierarchy items can't be easily adapted to a real-life situation, modify them so they can. Consider the item: "Elevator stuck between floors." This is clearly something you can't create on demand. But you can modify it to: "Standing in the elevator where the door closes and it waits a *long* time before the elevator starts to rise." This isn't the same as being stuck between floors, but it evokes some of the same feelings.

Relying on a Support Person

It's often very helpful to rely on a person you trust (such as your spouse, partner, or a friend) to accompany you on your forays into your phobia hierarchy when you first begin the process of real-life desensitization. Your support person can provide reassurance and safety, distraction (by talking with you), encouragement to persist, and praise for your incremental successes.

(This is the point to discuss who is going to be the support person for the client. Will you as therapist be accompanying the client to practice exposure during subsequent therapy sessions, or will they need to rely on a friend or family member to assist them? They are going to need such a person to accompany them, in any case, during assigned exposure practice sessions between therapy sessions. Is this a situation where the client feels confident they can handle exposure on their own? If the client *prefers* to undertake exposure without the aid of a support person, they should be encouraged to do so.)

Your support person should not push you. That person *should* encourage you to enter your phobic situation without running away. However, it's up to you to decide on the intensity of your exposure and to determine when you reach level 4 on the Anxiety Scale and need to temporarily back off—what we call "retreat." Your support person should not criticize your attempts or tell you to try harder. Yet it is good if she or he can identify any resistance on your part and help you to recognize whether such resistance is present. Your partner's main job is to provide encouragement and support without judging your performance. We will discuss guidelines for your support person in detail later.

Identifying Your Particular Sensitivities

As you undertake exposure, look for which particular characteristics of your phobic situation make you anxious. Some of these may correspond to the variables we discussed last week: spatial proximity, temporal proximity, duration of exposure, intensity of exposure, and degree of support. However, there may be other parameters unique to your particular phobia. For example, if driving freeways is a problem, the amount of traffic or lane you're in may affect your anxiety level. Becoming aware of the specific elements of your phobic situation that make you anxious will increase your sense of control over that situation and accelerate desensitization. You may want to make a list of your particular sensitivities for your phobia on the back of your hierarchy worksheet for that phobia.

Skill Building

Procedure for Exposure

It is important to follow these steps when you practice exposure to your phobic situation:

1. *Proceed into your phobic situation* (whatever step in your hierarchy you're on) *and stay there so long as your anxiety stays below level 4 on the Anxiety Scale*. In other words, keep going into or remain in the situation for at least one minute or to the point where your anxiety *first begins to feel unmanageable*. If you can stay in the situation for two or three minutes or longer, so much the better. While in the situation, use your anxiety management skills (abdominal breathing, coping statements, talking to your support person) to manage your anxiety. Even if you are uncomfortable in the situation, *stay with it* as long as your anxiety level does not go beyond moderate anxiety—level 3.

   If your anxiety does not go above a level 3 after two or three minutes, proceed to the next step up in your hierarchy. Then repeat step 1, staying in the situation for at least one minute or until your anxiety reaches level 4 on the Anxiety Scale. If your anxiety stays below level 4 for two to three minutes and you feel in control, proceed to the next step up in your hierarchy. Continue in this fashion for up to an hour. Longer exposure practice periods (i.e., one hour) are generally more effective than shorter periods.

You do not need to follow steps 2 through 5 so long as your anxiety stays manageable—below level 4.

Please Note: If your anxiety reaches or exceeds level 4 on the Anxiety Scale and you are *not* able to immediately retreat from the situation, practice your anxiety management skills (i.e., abdominal breathing, coping statements, talking to your support person, moving around if feasible) until retreat becomes possible. (If aboard an airplane, you need to reframe the idea of "retreat." Think of it as retreating to "a safe place in your mind." Realize that just as anxiety is created in your mind, so too can a sense of safety or safe place be created in your mind. Alternatively, try retreating to the rest room in the back of the plane.)

2. *Retreat*, temporarily, from the situation at any time where your anxiety reaches level 4 or *the point where it begins to feel not fully manageable*—the point where it feels like it might get out of control. Retreat means *temporarily* leaving the situation until you feel better and then *returning*. In most situations this is literally possible (when aboard an airplane, you can retreat to the rest room or to your peaceful scene in your mind). *Retreat is not the same as escaping or avoiding the situation*. It is designed to prevent you from "flooding" and risking the possibility of resensitizing yourself to the situation, which might reinforce the strength of your phobia.

   (**Note:** In most cases it is advisable to exercise the retreat option during exposure, rather than encouraging the client to endure the anxiety. If you as therapist prefer, however, to use an endurance approach to exposure (see page 8), then you might explain to the client that even though their anxiety rises above level 4 on the Anxiety Scale, it will eventually subside if they stay in the situation long enough. The one benefit of the endurance approach is that the client learns they can survive any level of anxiety and still handle the situation. This should be emphasized in defense of such an approach.)

3. *Recover*. After you temporarily pull back from your phobic situation, wait until your anxiety level diminishes to no more than level 1 or 2 on the Anxiety Scale. Be sure to give yourself sufficient time for your anxiety to subside. You may find that abdominal breathing or walking around at this point helps you recover your equanimity.

4. *Repeat*. After recovering, it is important to reenter your phobic situation and continue to stay with it so long as your anxiety remains below level 4 on the Anxiety Scale. Use your anxiety-management skills, as before. If you are able to go further or stay longer in the situation than you did before, fine. If not—or if you can't go even as far as you did the first time—that's fine, too. Do not chastise yourself if your performance after retreating turns out to be less spectacular than it was initially. This is a common experience. In a day or two you'll find that you'll be able to continue in your progression up your hierarchy.

5. *Continue going through the above cycle—Expose-Retreat-Recover-Repeat—*until you begin to feel tired or bored, then stop for the day. This constitutes one practice session, and it will typically take you from thirty minutes to two hours. For most people an hour-long practice session per day is enough. In your first session you may be unable to master the first step in your hierarchy or you may progress through the first four or five steps. *The limit for how far you go in any practice session should be determined by the point when your anxiety reaches level 4 on the Anxiety Scale.*

On some days you'll enjoy excellent progress, on others you'll hardly progress at all, and on still others you will not go as far as you did on preceding days. On a given Monday you might be able to ride an elevator up one floor. On Tuesday you can do the same thing but no more. Then on Wednesday you are unable to get on the elevator at all. Thursday or Friday, however, you may discover that you can go up two floors. This up-and-down, "two steps forward, one step back" phenomenon is typical of exposure therapy. Don't let it discourage you!

Guidelines for Undertaking Exposure

The following instructions are intended to help you get the most out of exposure:

1. *Be willing to take risks.*
   Entering a phobic situation that you've been avoiding for a long time is going to involve taking a mild to moderate risk. There's simply no risk-free way to face your fear and recover. Risk-taking is easier, however, when you start with small, limited goals and proceed incrementally. Establishing a hierarchy of exposures allows you to take this incremental approach.

2. *Deal with resistance.*
   Undertaking exposure to a situation that you've been avoiding may bring up resistance. Notice if you delay getting started with your exposure sessions or find reasons to procrastinate. The mere thought of actually entering your phobic situation may elicit strong anxiety, a fear of being trapped, or self-defeating statements to yourself such as, "I'll never be able to do it," or "This is hopeless." Instead of getting stuck in resistance, try to regard the process of desensitization as a major therapeutic opportunity. By plunging in you will learn about yourself and work through long-standing avoidance patterns that have held up your life. Give yourself pep talks about how much your life will improve when you are no longer held back by your phobia.

   Once you get through any initial resistance to real-life exposure, the going gets easier. If you have problems with resistance, we will talk about it next time.

3. *Be willing to tolerate some discomfort.*
   Facing a situation that you've been avoiding for a long time is not particularly comfortable or pleasant. It's inevitable and, in fact, necessary that you experience some anxiety in the course of becoming desensitized. It is com-

mon to feel *worse initially* at the outset of exposure therapy before you feel better. Recognize that feeling worse is not an indication of regression but rather that exposure is really working. Feeling worse means that you're laying the foundation to feel better. As you gain more skill in handling symptoms of anxiety when they come up during exposure, your practice sessions will become easier and you'll gain more confidence about following through to completion.

You may find the following affirmation helpful when you feel anxious: "This anxiety (or discomfort) means I'm already beginning to desensitize," or "Anxiety means that desensitization is in progress."

4. *Avoid flooding—be willing to retreat.*

Your exposure sessions are entirely different from occasions where you are forced to be in your phobic situation. In the process of exposure, you are in control of the intensity and length of time you confront the situation—circumstance does not offer this luxury. Always be willing to retreat from a practice situation if your anxiety reaches level 4 on the Anxiety Scale. Then wait until you recover before confronting your phobic situation again. *Retreat is not cowardly*—it is the most efficient and expedient way to master a phobia. Overexposure or flooding may resensitize you to a situation and ultimately prolong the time it takes to overcome your phobia. (**Note:** Omit this step if using an endurance approach to exposure.)

5. *Refine your hierarchy, if needed.*

If you have a problem getting beyond a particular step in your hierarchy, try going back to the preceding step for your next practice session and work your way back up. For example, if you've mastered driving over a small bridge but have difficulty advancing to the next largest one, go back and repeat driving over the smaller bridge several times. The object is to get so bored with the smaller bridge that you feel a strong incentive to attempt the next step up in your hierarchy. When you do, have your support person go with you. If possible, add an intermediate step when you have difficulty advancing from one step to the next.

If you have difficulty getting started with exposure therapy, try beginning with an even less challenging step than your original first step. For example, you might have a phobia about flying and you don't feel ready even to drive to the airport. As a preliminary step, watch a video that shows jets taking off and in flight, or get used to looking at photos of planes in a magazine. If you still can't make it to the airport, drive *by* it repeatedly until you feel able to drive to the airport parking lot, turn around, and return home.

6. *Plan "escape routes."*

Suppose you're practicing on an elevator and the worst happens—it stops between floors. Or suppose you are beginning to drive on the freeway and you start to panic when you're far away from an exit. It's good to plan ahead for worst-case scenarios whenever possible. In the first example, give yourself some insurance by practicing on an elevator that has a functioning emergency phone. Or in the case of the freeway, tell yourself in advance that it will be all right to retreat to the shoulder or at least drive slowly with your emergency flashers on until you reach an exit. *Be aware of your escape routes or "trap doors" in advance of exposure to your phobia.* Knowing that you have an escape route will help make exposure easier.

7. *Trust your own pace.*

   It's important not to regard real-life exposure as some kind of race. The goal is not to see how fast you can overcome your problem: pressuring yourself to make great strides quickly is generally not a good idea. In fact doing so carries a risk of resensitizing yourself to your phobia if you attempt advanced steps in your hierarchy before becoming fully comfortable with earlier steps. Decide on the pace you wish to adopt in exposing yourself to a difficult situation, realizing that very small gains count for a lot in this type of work.

8. *Reward yourself for your successes.*

   It's common for people going through exposure to castigate themselves for not making sufficiently rapid progress. Bear in mind that it's important to consistently reward yourself for your successes, however small. For example, being able to go into your phobic situation further than the day before is worthy of giving yourself a reward, such as a new piece of clothing or dinner out. So is being able to stay in the situation a few moments longer—or being able to tolerate anxious feelings a few moments longer. Rewarding yourself for your successes will help sustain your motivation to keep practicing. After a while your successes may become inherently rewarding.

9. *Use anxiety management strategies.*

   Whenever anxiety begins to come on, use the anxiety management skills you have been practicing:

   - Abdominal breathing
   - Coping statements (use your list or three-by-five cards)
   - Moving around
   - Conversation with your support person
   - Distractions (such as counting the number of red cars on the freeway)
   - Anger (get angry with your anxiety)

   Remember to maintain an overall attitude of "acceptance" and "going with" any uncomfortable body sensations rather than balking or resisting them. Using abdominal breathing and coping statements in combination often helps.

10. *Practice regularly.*

    Methodical and regular practice—rather than hurrying or pressuring yourself—will do the most to expedite overcoming your fear. Ideally it is good to practice real-life exposure *three to five times per week.* Longer practice sessions, with several trials of exposure to your phobic situation, tend to be more effective than briefer sessions. As long as you retreat when appropriate, it's impossible to undergo too much exposure in a given practice session (the worst that can happen is that you might end up somewhat tired or drained).

The *regularity* of your practice will determine the rate of your recovery. If you find it difficult to practice regularly, we will discuss what kinds of resistance or other issues might be getting in your way. *Regular practice of exposure is the key to getting over your phobia.* It is the strongest predictor of your eventual success with exposure.

11. *Expect and know how to handle setbacks.*

Not being able to tolerate as much exposure to a situation as you did previously is a normal part of recovery. Recovery simply doesn't proceed in a linear fashion—there will be plateaus and regressions as well as times of moving forward. *Setbacks are an integral part of the recovery process.*

For example, suppose you are working on overcoming a phobia about driving on the freeway. Your practice sessions over a four-week period might go like this:

Week 1: During three out of five practice sessions you can drive the distance of one exit on the freeway.

Week 2: For five out of five practice sessions you can't get on the freeway at all. (This degree of regression is not at all uncommon.)

Week 3: For two out of five practice sessions you are able to drive the distance of one exit. During two other sessions you're able to drive the distance of two exits. One day you can't get on the freeway at all.

Week 4: Due to illness you only get in two practice sessions. On one of those days you're able to manage three exits, on the other day you go one exit.

It's very important not to let a setback discourage you from further practice. Simply chalk it up to a bad day or bad week and learn from it. Nothing can take away the progress you've made up to that point. You can use each setback as a learning experience to tell you more about how to best proceed in mastering your phobic situation. *Your ability to tolerate setbacks and still persist with your daily practice sessions is a crucial determinant of your success.*

12. *Follow through to completion.*

Finishing exposure means that you reach a point where you no longer avoid your phobic situation *and* are not afraid of anxiety whenever you confront that situation. You will need to keep exposing to the situation many times to reach a point where you are no longer anxious there. It is important not to stop short of this, not to give up before you are essentially free of anxiety in the situation. If you master your phobia to this level, you'll be unlikely to have it come up again in the future.

Summary of Session

(as in session 2)

Feedback from Client

(as in session 2)

Homework

1. Review the section "Procedure for Exposure" so that you're thoroughly familiar with the correct procedure for real-life desensitization. Learning to retreat and recover when your anxiety reaches level 4 on the Anxiety Scale is especially important.

2. Review the section "Guidelines for Undertaking Exposure" so that you fully understand all of the ingredients that contribute to success with real-life desensitization. Your willingness to deal with initial resistance, tolerate some discomfort, learn to retreat, practice regularly, and handle setbacks is particularly important.

3. Find a relative or friend who is willing to work with you as a support person. Bring them to the following session. (**Note:** If neither a friend or relative is available, you may need to hire someone.)

4. Continue working up your imagery desensitization hierarchy, practicing at least three times this week.

5. Continue working with abdominal breathing and progressive muscle relaxation on a daily basis. Practice your worry-management skills as needed. Reframe negative self-talk using the Worry Worksheet if anticipatory anxiety becomes particularly bothersome.

Session 6—Main Points

- Explain the nature and rationale of exposure, the principal method for treating specific phobia.

- Have the client construct an exposure hierarchy for their phobia (utilizing their imagery desensitization hierarchy as a basis).

- Review with the client what particular parameters of their phobic situation tend to make them more or less anxious. These should be reflected in the hierarchy.

- Discuss whether the client will be using a support person for exposure and who that person is going to be.

- Go over the procedure for exposure in detail.

- Discuss all of the *guidelines* for undertaking exposure in detail. Make sure the client understands the import of each of the guidelines.

- Homework Assignments.

Session 7

Educating the Client's Support Person for Exposure

Monitoring of Current Status

(as in session 2)

Agenda

The purpose of this session is to begin conducting real-life exposure with the client. If it is impractical for you as therapist to accompany the client, then this week's session is devoted to training the client's support person to do so. Even if you are conducting exposure, the support person should attend this session and accompany the client on the first live exposure outing. This is the best way to educate the support person about how to work with the client during "homework" exposure practice between therapy sessions. If neither the therapist nor client have much "hands-on" experience with exposure, it is important to follow the "Procedure for Direct Exposure" (presented in last week's session) carefully. The client needs to stay with the initial exposure (the first step in the hierarchy) for at least one to three minutes, so long as anxiety does not exceed what the client has deemed "level 3" on the Anxiety Scale. If anxiety rises to or exceeds level 4, it's critical for the client to retreat and then return to the phobic situation after recovering. Frequently clients do not want to retreat, or they do retreat and then do not want to return to their phobic situation. In the first instance, you need to reinforce the idea that retreating is not a sign of weakness or failure, but a necessary part of the exposure procedure. After retreating, the client may need some encouragement to return to the situation. Emphasize the point that they can only unlearn their avoidance pattern by returning to the situation after retreat. Returning to the situation may be difficult, yet it is simply the best way to gain confidence that they can truly handle a situation they have previously avoided.

The first exposure session may need to be short, since the client may tire rather quickly when attempting to confront their phobia for the first time. It's common to spend only a half-hour to forty-five minutes doing a first exposure. Later, exposure sessions can be extended to an hour or, if feasible, to ninety minutes.

Review of Homework

Ask the client if they have any remaining questions regarding the procedure or guidelines for undertaking exposure. Have they brought a friend or relative with them who can accompany them during exposure practice sessions?

Psychoeducation

The guidelines presented below, while intended for training the client's support person, are obviously pertinent to any therapist inexperienced in conducting exposure sessions. All of the guidelines are important, but pay attention particularly to numbers 4 and 10. While it is important to offer the client a lot of encouragement, it's equally important not to push them during exposure. For the client to gain a sense of mastery, it's critical that they feel in control and set both the pace and limits of any given exposure session.

Guidelines for The Support Person

Go over these guidelines, one by one, with both the client and support person.

1. Be familiar with the process of exposure in overcoming phobias. See the client manual or chapter 8 of *The Anxiety and Phobia Workbook* (1995).

2. Before beginning a practice session, communicate clearly with your phobic partner about what they expect of you during practice. Do they want you to talk a lot to them? Stay right with them? Follow behind them? Wait outside? Hold their hand?

3. If your partner is easily overwhelmed, help them to break exposure down into small, incremental steps.

4. It's up to the phobic—not the support person—to define the goals of a given practice session. As a support person, be encouraging and cooperative rather than assuming the initiative.

5. Be familiar with the phobic's early warning signs of anxiety. Encourage them to *verbalize when they're beginning to feel overly anxious* (reaching level

4 on the Anxiety Scale). Don't be afraid to ask them from time to time how they're doing.

6. Be familiar with your partner's coping statements and other anxiety-management procedures. Remind them to use these techniques during exposure.

7. Don't allow your partner's distress to rattle you, but don't fail to take it seriously. Remember that anxiety isn't necessarily rational. In case of a full-blown panic attack, quietly lead your partner away from the threatening situation, end the practice session for the day, and take them home. Above all, stay close by until the panic completely subsides.

8. A hug can go much further than a lot of words. If you see that your partner is frightened in a particular situation, your hug or the offer of your hand will help relieve anxiety better than any lecture about how there is no reason to be afraid.

9. Be reliable. Be where you say you're going to be during a practice session. Don't move to another location because you want to test your partner. It can be very frightening for the phobic to return to a prearranged meeting place and find you gone.

10. *Don't push a person with phobias!* Phobics know what's going on in their body and may panic if pushed further than they're ready to go at a particular point in exposure.

11. On the other hand, encourage your partner to make the most out of practice. It's better to attempt to enter a frightening situation and have to retreat than not to try at all. Your partner's resistance may be making practice impossible or may be impeding progress. If your partner seems stalled or unmotivated to practice, ask what is getting in the way of proceeding. Assist, if you can, in exploring and identifying psychological resistance.

12. In spite of all your desire to help, phobics must assume responsibility for their own recovery. Be supportive and encouraging but avoid trying to step in and do it all for them. This will only undermine their confidence.

13. Try to see things from the phobic's standpoint. Things which seem insignificant to others—such as riding a bus or eating in a restaurant—may involve a great deal of work and courage for the phobic to achieve, even for a short period of time. These accomplishments and the efforts leading to them should be recognized.

14. Phobics generally are very sensitive and respond well to praise, even for small achievements. Praise them for whatever they accomplish and be understanding and accepting when they regress.

15. Encourage practice with rewards. For example, you might say, "When you can handle restaurants, let's have lunch together somewhere special."

16. Accept the phobic's "bad" day and reinforce the idea that they can't have a perfect day every time. Backsliding and setbacks are part of the normal course of exposure therapy.

17. It may be necessary to readjust your own schedule to effectively help your partner. Be sure you're willing to make a commitment to work with your partner regularly over a sustained period of time before offering to be a support person. If you're unable to see them through the full period of recovery (which can take several months or longer), let them know specifically how long a commitment you can make.

18. Know your own limits. Be forgiving when you are a less than perfect support person. If your capacity to be supportive has been stretched to the limit, take a break.

Summary of Session

(as in session 2)

Feedback from Client

After answering questions either the client or support person might have about the preceding guidelines, set a goal for exposure for the following week. Let the *client* decide what they feel would be a reasonable goal to attempt (for example, the first three steps in their hierarchy). *It is not critical that the client actually achieve the designated goal so much as that they have something in mind to aim for.*

Homework

1. Practice real-life exposure in an effort to reach the assigned goal for next week. The goal is defined in terms of a particular level in the client's hierarchy. Practice a minimum of three times for up to an hour during the week, preferably more.

2. Utilize anxiety management skills (breathing, coping statements, etc.) both during as well as between exposure practice sessions, whenever physical symptoms of anxiety arise. Continue to use worry-management techniques to handle anticipatory anxiety (worry).

3. Identify, challenge, and counter negative self-talk around facing your phobia at least once during the week using the Worry Worksheet.

4. Continue progressive muscle relaxation and imagery desensitization if unfinished with your imagery hierarchy.

Session 7—Main Points

- Conduct initial exposure with the client outside the office and/or educate the client's support person about how to assist the client (the support person should participate in this session either way).

- Make sure the client appreciates the importance of retreating at any time their anxiety exceeds level 3 on the Anxiety Scale. This is best taught during exposure itself.

- Set a goal for exposure that the client is to practice at home for the following week.

- Homework Assignments.

Session 8

Evaluating the First Attempt at Exposure

Monitoring of Current Status

(as in session 2)

Agenda

If you as therapist are conducting exposure, this session is devoted to continuing with exposure to higher levels in the client's hierarchy. If a support person is working with the client outside of therapy, this week can be devoted to reviewing how the initial exposure efforts went, addressing any problems that arose.

Review of Homework

Ask the client how their practice exposure sessions went. How far did they progress up their hierarchy? If you are not accompanying the client with exposure this session, proceed with the agenda below. If you are doing exposure this session, allow time to discuss any problems that came up with practice sessions at home before going out to practice.

Concepts and Skills

Psychoeducation

Obstacles to making progress with exposure may come up in any of the following five areas.

Resistance

Resistance is usually evident when the client skips or procrastinates in doing regular exposure sessions at home. Statements such as "I'm not in the mood," "I just didn't feel like it," "I'll do it next time (later, tomorrow, etc.)" are common. Rather than being confrontational, it is best to normalize resistance. You might say for example:

"It's common to have difficulty in undertaking exposure. After all, you have been avoiding your phobic situation for a long time. In facing it, you risk having anxiety come up. In fact, some anxiety is inevitable in undertaking exposure. This anxiety can be minimized by breaking the task of exposure down into a number of manageable steps and working with your support person. Even so, it's likely you may have some anxiety. Exposure is not a comfortable process; it is hard work. The reward of doing that work is that you overcome your phobia. You have to decide whether the prospect of being free of your phobia is important enough to justify putting in the work and experiencing the discomfort that's involved. I will help you in every way I can, but ultimately the decision is up to you. Undertaking exposure—facing what you fear—is the only way you are likely to overcome it."

High Anxiety

The client begins exposure, but experiences high anxiety or panic from the very beginning.

- Break down the first step of the hierarchy into smaller steps. For example, instead of getting on board the elevator, repeat walking up and merely looking at an elevator many times. Instead of going to the airport terminal, drive by it a number of times.

- Spend the first few exposure sessions doing nothing other than retreating and returning. Enter the phobic situation to a very minimal degree for a short time, then back off and relax. When you're recovered, repeat the minimal exposure, followed by retreat. After an hour of small exposures alternating with retreats, you may be ready to increase the extent or duration of your exposure.

- If neither of these adjustments to the procedure work, consider taking a low dose of a benzodiazepine tranquilizer. Do this with the approval of your doctor, and *only* when undertaking exposure. A low dose (for example 0.25 mg Xanax or Ativan) is necessary because you don't want to mask anxiety altogether during exposure. It is necessary to feel some anxiety for desensitization to occur.

Difficulty Progressing

If the client is having trouble moving past a particular step in the hierarchy, add an intermediate step, if possible. For example, if you watched someone else get an injection but are not ready to get one yourself, have the nurse let you handle (or take home) a syringe so that you can practice putting the needle up to your skin on your own (preferably without puncturing the skin).

If an intermediate step is not possible, then wait until the "right" day to attempt the next step in your hierarchy. For example, you might be trying to progress in exposure to a longer bridge, and the increase in length or height of the next bridge seems too great. Wait until you feel highly motivated to attempt the larger bridge. Ordinarily, it is important *not* to delay exposure practice until you feel like it. You will desensitize more effectively if you resolve to practice three times per week regardless of how you are feeling. However, in moving up a difficult step in your hierarchy, it may be advisable to wait until you feel motivated to attempt it (with your support person). An alternative approach is to rely on medication, as described previously.

Setbacks

A setback occurs when the client has been progressing and suddenly is unable to go as far or stay as long with exposure as during the previous or recent practice sessions.

There is nothing wrong with setbacks; *they are a normal and expected part of exposure.* The important thing is how you handle them. Keep three things in mind.

First, setbacks are normal. They happen to *everyone* undertaking exposure. The course of exposure is hardly ever linear; it is fraught with ups and downs—two steps forward, one step back. The fact that you had a setback means you are actually practicing exposure and making headway.

Second, setbacks are always temporary, provided you resolve to go forward. You do *not* lose the ground you've gained prior to the setback—it may just seem like that temporarily. When the setback passes, you will resume from where you left off in a short time if you keep practicing.

Third, it is important to view any setback not as a defeat but as an opportunity to learn. When you understand the circumstances that caused the setback, you may be able to avoid repeating those circumstances in the future. The greatest opportunity afforded by a setback is the chance to build confidence in mastering your fear. Nothing builds confidence like being able to pass through a setback and continue on your way toward your goal. However discouraging a setback may seem initially, it is always an opportunity to gain strength and confidence in your eventual success.

Secondary Gains

Secondary gains are unconscious reasons you might want to hold on to your phobia. This idea may at first seem preposterous. You protest that you want nothing more than to be free of your fear. Certainly you believe you did not develop your phobia in order to gain some hidden benefit.

Most likely your phobia did not develop out of a desire to meet some unconscious need. However, once you have the phobia, it *may* offer certain benefits or fulfill some needs. The gain you receive did not motivate or cause the phobia, it is *secondary* to it. For example, if being phobic of driving means your spouse has to take over all of your children's transportation needs, you may be relieved of something you would prefer not to do even if you could drive. The benefits of not driving may subtly interfere with your progress toward regaining that capacity.

Another secondary gain is being able to avoid the unknown. On an unconscious level, you may be so familiar with the restrictions caused by your phobia that the idea of being totally free of them is a bit scary. The "terrible known" is more comfortable than an unknown that promises to be better.

If you believe there might be secondary gains interfering with your progress in exposure, it is important to examine what they might be. Even if it initially seems ridiculous, take some time to really think about what benefits or advantages you might get from keeping your phobia. Is there anything you would be giving up if you were completely free of your fear? Then reflect about this not only for yourself but for your spouse and immediate family. Are *they* getting any benefits by your remaining phobic? How would it affect them if you were free of your fear?

Your ability to completely overcome your phobia will be enhanced by both your awareness and willingness to relinquish any secondary gains.

Summary of Session

(as in session 2)

Feedback from Client

(as in session 2)

Homework

For this week, homework includes:

1. Practice exposure (with your support person or alone) at least three separate times during the week.

2. Utilize anxiety management skills in advance of and during exposure practices.

3. Identify, challenge, and counter negative self-statements contributing to anticipatory anxiety at least once during the week, preferably at a time when you are relaxed and can think through the process clearly.

Session 8—Main Points

- Review how the client's initial practice with exposure went.

- Continue *in vivo* exposure (therapist-assisted exposure), if feasible.

- Explore any resistance (including secondary gains) that the client has to practicing exposure.

- Address any problems that occur during the course of exposure, such as high anxiety, difficulty progressing beyond a certain level in the hierarchy, or early setbacks.

- Ask the client how they feel about their support person; address any issues.

- Homework Assignments.

Session 9

Continue (or Review) Exposure Practice

Monitoring of Current Status

(as in session 2)

Agenda

The primary agenda for this session is to prepare for the completion of treatment after ten sessions *or* to arrange for therapy to continue beyond ten sessions. If the client's resources are limited, then it's critical at this point to discuss how exposure work can continue after therapy—either with a support person or alone. In many cases, clients do need to continue with exposure practice beyond ten therapy sessions to fully overcome and master a specific phobia. It is a good idea, if possible, to arrange for a follow-up session approximately one month after the tenth session to evaluate how the client is doing. I also like to give the client the option of calling me if they run into a major setback or obstacle in proceeding up through their exposure hierarchy. Even though the basic therapy program is complete, this offers the client continued support until they reach their goal.

If possible, it is preferable for the client to continue with treatment beyond ten sessions until they have fully mastered their phobia. If the therapist is doing exposure with the client, each weekly session is devoted to exposure practice until the client is able to fully confront their phobic situation with minimal anxiety. This can require a total of twenty or more sessions in some cases. If the client is working with a support person, therapy sessions are devoted to monitoring progress with exposure, troubleshooting problems that come up and, in the time remaining, exploring any *other* issues the client would like to address apart from their specific phobia. If the client has no concerns beyond their phobia, therapy sessions can be limited to a half-hour at this point.

In any case, by the end of the ninth session, both therapist and client should have a clear idea about whether: 1) treatment will be completed the following week (with the option of a one-month follow-up session and/or follow-up phone calls), or 2) treatment will continue beyond the tenth session, with either the therapist or a support person seeing the client through to the completion of exposure. After this discussion, the rest of the session is devoted either to exposure or any questions, needs, or concerns the client has regarding their exposure work with their support person. Any obstacles or problems are explored in the same way they were in session 8.

Review of Homework

Evaluate the client's progress with *in vivo* exposure. Discuss any continuing sources of resistance and/or setbacks.

Summary of Session

(as in session 2)

Feedback from Client

(as in session 2)

Homework

Homework for this week includes:

1. Continue to practice exposure (with support person or alone) at least three times during the week.

2. Utilize anxiety and worry management skills both in advance of and during exposure practices.

3. Identify, challenge, and counter any negative self-talk contributing to anticipatory anxiety at least once during the week. As in the preceding week, this should be done at a time when you are relaxed and can think through the process clearly.

Session 9—Main Points

- Discuss the client's plans for continuing therapy beyond ten sessions.

- If therapy is to end after ten sessions, arrange for follow-up of the client's progress either by phone or in an actual follow-up session.

- Continue exposure practice with the client if feasible.

- Continue to evaluate the client's progress with exposure practice, addressing resistance or any other problems that arise (as is session 8).

- Homework Assignments.

Session 10

Final Session

Monitoring of Current Status

(as in session 2)

Agenda

For some clients this may be the final session. If so, the session needs to focus on three themes: 1) summarizing progress to date, 2) discussing strategies for relapse prevention, and 3) achieving closure.

Review of Homework

Evaluate the client's progress with exposure.

Concepts and Skills

Evaluating Progress

In summarizing progress, ask the client to make an estimate of how far they feel they have progressed toward overcoming their phobia. Are they satisfied with their progress to date? Are they satisfied with the therapy in general—or is there something they wish had happened that didn't? Are they willing to make a commitment following the final therapy session to continue with exposure until they reach their goal? Would they like to be able to call the therapist to report progress or any obstacles that arise? Would they like to have a follow-up session in one or two months? This is the point to have them complete the Program Satisfaction Questionnaire (see page 24). They should also complete the Fear Questionnaire (see page 15) at this time to evaluate symptom improvement since the first session.

Minimizing Relapse

There are two things to be mindful of in minimizing the prospect of relapse. First, the client needs to be aware that resistance to doing regular exposure practice may occur when he or she doesn't have the support of weekly therapy sessions. It's important to notice any procrastination or delay in getting started with exposure practice sessions—the proverbial "I'll do it tomorrow." If this gets to be a problem, the client should work it through with their support person or call the therapist. Second, if the client desires to fully master their phobic situation, all supports need eventually to be relinquished. It is the support person that is usually the first to go; exposure isn't complete until the client can handle their previously avoided situation alone. Each hierarchy step that was handled with the help of a support person needs to be negotiated alone.

The way I prefer to wean clients off their support person is to encourage them first to try early steps in their hierarchy alone while still negotiating more advanced steps (i.e., the last three or four steps) with their support person. In short, they are to practice, in any given week, at two different points in their hierarchy, one with support and the other alone. If a hierarchy has twelve steps, they should begin trying out steps 1 or 2 alone when they've reached steps 8 or 9 with support. For example, when a client has reached the point where they can ride an elevator to the fortieth floor of a sixty-floor building, they need to begin working on the first two or three floors alone. If this is too demanding, they might phase out reliance on their support person as follows: 1) the support person waits at the second floor while the client rides the elevator alone, 2) the support person waits at the ground level while the client ascends to the second floor and returns, and 3) the support person waits in a car outside the building. Similarly, for a fear of driving freeways, the support person might: 1) follow in a second car, 2) follow a few hundred yards behind in a second car, 3) wait at the destination, 4) wait at the point of origin, and 5) be available by cellular phone. By the time the client has successfully negotiated the highest and last step of their hierarchy with support, they should be well on their way to progressing up the earlier steps on their own.

Beyond the support person are all the other types of supports that can assist exposure in the early stages, including medications, cellular phones, lucky charms, and various distraction techniques. If the client needs to rely on such "safety signals" to handle their phobic situation, they run the risk of having anxiety crop up should they ever be suddenly faced with the situation without such devices being available. Relying on supports to handle a phobia is all right if all the client desires is to cope. However, full mastery of a phobia, with minimal risk of relapse, requires facing the situation repeatedly without supports.

A final important consideration in minimizing relapse is that the client continue to practice all of the anxiety and worry management techniques they have learned, particularly abdominal breathing and the use of coping statements. This is necessary both at the time of practicing exposure as well as any other times when anticipatory anxiety comes up. Reiterate that following through with exposure to completion is the best way to dispense with anticipatory anxiety.

Having discussed the importance of following through with exposure to completion, as well as ways to minimize possible relapse, it is time to bring therapy to a conclusion. This is the time to validate the client for all their hard work and to reiterate the offer of continuing support (by telephone or follow-up sessions) should difficulties arise. It is important also to offer encouragement and optimism about the client being able to fully reach their goal. Practicing exposure *will* enable them to fully desensitize to their phobia if they continue to put in the time and effort to practice.

I personally like to finish the session by thanking the client for giving me the opportunity to work with them.

Appendix 1

Special Considerations

Fear of Flying

Treating fear of flying has certain unique obstacles that deserve special attention. First, in most cases, clients present with more than one specific fear. It is common for a client to have two or three separate phobias, for example, fear of the plane crashing, fear of heights, and/or fear of confinement for a protracted period of time. It's necessary to address mistaken beliefs and unhelpful self-talk respective to each of these issues. Also, in most cases, it's advisable to work with a separate imagery desensitization hierarchy for each specific fear.

Second, the therapist often has to make a special effort to overcome the client's lopsided perception of the risk of flying. The tendency to dramatically overestimate the risk of flying comes from a reduced perception of control. By its very nature, flying involves relinquishing some degree of control—i.e., there is no way to physically exit a plane in flight and there is no way to see how the plane is being operated since passengers cannot enter the cockpit. Driving a car *appears* to be much safer because you are free to pull over in the event of trouble, and you are also in charge of operating the vehicle. I find that presenting the client with fatality and injury statistics for flying vs. driving is one way to begin to restructure their perception of risk.

It is also important to request that the client *not* expose themselves to media coverage of plane crashes on TV or in newspapers. Once again, this tends to falsely inflate their perception of risk. After they have become able to fly, watching media coverage of plane disasters may be attempted as a final "over-exposure" to ensure full mastery of their fear. However, I don't recommend it in general because of the media's tendency to sensationalize an event that kills far fewer people than many other causes of death that do not receive publicity.

Another problem with fear of flying is the difficulty of achieving gradual exposure. Often the client has to jump from imagery desensitization to an actual flight without any intermediate steps. There are two ways to overcome this issue. First, it may be possible to arrange with local airlines to have clients board a grounded plane. When I practiced in the San Francisco Bay area, I was able to make such an arrangement with Alaska Airlines. It helped clients considerably in making the transition from imagery practice to a real-life flight. The other possibility, which has worked well in some cases, is to have the client make short flights in a small plane with a private flying instructor. This is done prior to making their first commercial flight. Under these circumstances, the client is able to exercise some control over the duration and altitude of the flight and more gradually progress up to a situation that resembles a (short) commercial flight.

Finally, *mastery* of the fear of flying is generally costly. After making their first flight, the client needs to continue with exposure to flying to assure full mastery and minimize the risk of relapse. I recommend that clients make at least one flight every two or three months following their first flight for at least one year. Ideally, these flights should gradually increase in duration. The client should have a support person accompany them until they feel fully ready to attempt a flight on their own (preferably with the availability of a cellular phone).

A full discussion of the issues involved in treating fear of flying is beyond the scope of this manual. The reader is referred to the book *Flying Without Fear* (1996) by Duane Brown, Ph.D. (available at: [800] 748-6273) or the book-tape program *Achieving Comfortable Flight* by Reid Wilson, Ph.D., and Captain T.W. Cummings (available at [800] 394-2299).

Blood-Injury Phobia

What distinguishes blood-injury phobias from other specific phobias is the tendency of clients to faint upon the sight of blood (or receiving an injection). Using abdominal breathing or coping statements will manage anxiety but will not ordinarily offset a fainting response.

To minimize fainting, an intervention is added to prevent a precipitous drop in blood pressure. The client is taught to tense all of the muscles in his or her body for ten seconds. After tensing, the muscles are relaxed for ten seconds. Then this tense-relax sequence is repeated four or five more times. The client learns this simple technique (in addition to abdominal breathing and progressive muscle relaxation) in session 2. They are then given the additional homework assignment of practicing the tense-relax exercise (five repetitions each time) at least five times per day. Sessions 5–9 proceed as follows:

- Session 5: Have the client do the tense-relax exercise in session, followed by exposure to pictures of people with bloody injuries or persons receiving injections. Conduct imagery desensitization to the first two or three scenes in the client's hierarchy.

- Session 6: In addition to a full explanation of exposure, make an arrangement with a local hospital so that you and the client can go watch people get blood drawn. This arrangement can be made during the session.

- Session 7: Field trip to the hospital; the client watches patients having blood drawn, *after* practicing the tense-relax exercise.

- Session 8: The client has their own blood drawn, accompanied by the therapist or a support person.

- Session 9: The client has their own blood drawn, with their support person staying in the waiting room or absent altogether. (This exposure should be repeated three times to assure full mastery.)

Aversive Imagery

Aversive imagery is a variation on systematic desensitization. I have used it primarily with phobias of vomiting or of natural disasters, both situations where it is difficult to do real-life exposure. The procedure involves having the client write a very detailed script of the worst-case scenario regarding their phobia. For example, with a fear of vomiting, such a script might involve throwing up all over oneself at a formal dinner. The script is then recorded on a continuous loop tape. The client is instructed to listen to the tape every day until he or she desensitizes to the content. This may take numerous exposures, but the end result is that the client's fearful images associated with their phobia tend to lose their charge. When the worst case scenario is too anxiety-provoking, I ask the client to develop a hierarchy of scenes progressing up to the worst. Each scene is written out in detail, recorded on a continuous loop tape, and then confronted repeatedly. As a general rule, aversive imagery is effective only when the client is willing to do many exposures. This requires a genuine commitment on the client's part, since exposure to a worst-case scene can be quite unpleasant initially.

The interested reader is referred to the audio tape "Acquiring Courage" by Zev Wanderer for a more detailed presentation of this technique (see appendix 3).

Examples of Hierarchies

Driving With a Partner as Passenger

1. Sit in a car for one to five minutes with your partner in the passenger seat.

2. Drive one block making smooth stops and starts.

3. Drive in a residential area making right turns.

4. Drive in a residential area making left turns.

5. Drive in the right lane of a minor arterial.

6. Drive on a minor arterial making left turns at a stop sign or traffic light.

7. Drive on a major arterial in the right lane.

8. Drive on a major arterial, changing lanes, and making left and U-turns.

9. Drive on the freeway in the right lane for one to two exits.

10. Drive on the freeway, changing lanes and passing cars for two to five exits.

Driving Alone

When you practice driving alone, first have your partner follow you in another car as you go through the steps. When you feel comfortable, have your partner drive ahead of you in another car. When you're comfortable with this, then practice by yourself.

1. Sit in the car for one to five minutes alone.

2. Drive one block making smooth stops and starts.

3. Drive in a residential area making right turns.

4. Drive in a residential area making left turns.

5. Drive in the right lane of a minor arterial.

6. Drive on a minor arterial making left turns at a stop sign or traffic light.

7. Drive on a major arterial in the right lane.

8. Drive on a major arterial, changing lanes and making left and U-turns.

9. Drive on the freeway in the right lane for one or two exits.

10. Drive on the freeway, changing lanes and passing cars for two to five exits.

Heights

1. Look out the window of a one-story building for ten to sixty seconds.

2. With your partner, look out a second-story window for thirty to sixty seconds.

3. With your partner, look out a second-story window for two to five minutes; look straight ahead and then down.

4. Look out a second-story window alone for thirty to sixty seconds; look straight ahead and then down.

5. With your partner, look out a third-story window for one to two minutes; look straight ahead and then down.

6. Look out a third-story window alone for one to two minutes; look straight ahead and then down.

7. With your partner, look out a fourth-story window for one to two minutes; look straight ahead and then down.

8. Look out a fourth-story window alone for two to five minutes; look straight ahead and then down.

9. With your partner, look out from an open area (i.e. a fire escape or balcony) of a five- to ten-story building, trying each floor from the fifth floor to the tenth; look straight ahead and then down at each level.

10. Without your partner, look out from an open area of a five- to ten-story building, trying each floor from the fifth to the tenth; look straight ahead and then down at each level.

Elevators

1. Approach an elevator with your partner; look at it, and then retreat.

2. Walk with your partner into an elevator with the door remaining open (have your partner make sure the door remains open).

3. Walk with your partner into an elevator and allow the door to close.

4. With your partner, ride up one floor.

5. With your partner, ride up two or more floors.

6. Ride up two or more floors with your partner waiting at the floor where you exit the elevator.

7. Ride up two or more floors with your partner waiting for you on the ground floor.

8. Ride the elevator while your partner is somewhere else in the building.

9. Ride the elevator alone for two or more floors without your partner being available.

10. Ride a less familiar elevator alone, without your partner being available.

Buses and Trains

This hierarchy is described for buses but can be used in the same manner for trains.

1. With your partner, ride on a bus for one stop, sitting on the aisle near the door.

2. With your partner, ride the bus for two to five stops, sitting on the aisle near the door.

3. With your partner, ride the bus for five or more stops, sitting in the back of the bus.

4. With your partner following in a car, ride the bus one stop, sitting on the aisle near the door.

5. With your partner following in a car, ride the bus for two to five stops, sitting on the aisle near the door.

6. With your partner following in a car, ride the bus five or more stops, sitting in the back of the bus.

7. Alone, without your partner following, ride the bus one stop, sitting on the aisle near the door.

8. Alone, without your partner following, ride the bus two to five stops, sitting on the aisle near the door.

9. Alone, without your partner following, ride the bus two to five stops, sitting in the back of the bus.

10. Alone, without your partner following, ride the bus more than five stops, sitting in the back of the bus.

Dentists and Doctors

This hierarchy is designed for people with a fear of dentists but can be used in the same manner for doctor phobias.

1. With your partner, walk in and out of a dentist's office.

2. With your partner, sit in the waiting room for two to five minutes.

3. With your partner, sit in the waiting room for ten to fifteen minutes.

4. Make an appointment with the dentist just to talk to him for five to ten minutes. Tell him about your problem and explain that you are trying to desensitize yourself. Ask for his cooperation.

5. With your partner, sit in the dentist's chair five to ten minutes without the dentist being in attendance, then leave.

6. With your partner, sit in the dentist's chair ten to twenty minutes without the dentist being in attendance, then leave.

7. Make an appointment with your dentist to just look in your mouth, and not to do any work, with your partner staying with you.

8. Make an appointment with your dentist to clean your teeth only, with your partner staying with you.

9. Make an appointment for the dentist to do more work while your partner is with you.

10. Repeat steps 7 through 9 without your partner.

Airports and Flying

1. Approach the airport with your partner and drive around it.

2. Park in the airport garage or lot; remain observing people for five minutes.

3. Park in the airport lot, enter the terminal with your partner, and remain one to five minutes.

4. Enter the terminal alone and remain five minutes, browsing and observing.

5. Arrange to visit a grounded plane; enter with your partner.

6. Enter a grounded plane alone and remain inside for five minutes.

7. Enter a grounded plane with your partner and get buckled into a seat. Remain five minutes.

8. Enter a grounded plane alone, browse, and then stay buckled into a seat for ten to fifteen minutes.

9. Schedule a short flight (ten to thirty minutes) and go with your partner.

10. Schedule a longer flight and go with your partner.

11. Repeat steps 9 and 10 alone.

Resources

I Can Do It tape series by Edmund Bourne, Ph.D., available from New Harbinger Publications at (800) 748-6273. (addresses specific phobias of flying, heights, contracting illness, driving freeways, grocery shopping, driving far from home, and public speaking)

Acquiring Courage by Zev Wanderer, Ph.D., available from New Harbinger Publications at (800) 748-6273. (aversive imagery)

Achieving Comfortable Flight by Reid Wilson, Ph.D., and Captain T. W. Cummings, available from Pathway Systems at (800) 394-2299.

Overcoming Driving Fears and Stress, I and II by Sy Cohn, MFCC, available at (800) 474-6242.

Appendix 4

Treatment Plan

Problem: Specific Phobia

Definition: A strong fear and avoidance of *one particular* type of object or situation, in this case _____. Confronting this object or situation provokes anxiety/dread and interferes with normal routines, work, or relationships.

Goals: Significant reduction in fear and avoidance behavior so that the client can function normally in proximity to the feared object or situation.

Objectives:	Interventions:
1. Develop stress management skills.	1. Teach abdominal breathing, progressive muscle relaxation, and relaxation imagery techniques.
2. Develop worry management skills.	2. Cognitive restructuring to confront overestimation of danger and underestimation of coping resources. Teach worry management and distraction techniques.
3. Develop anxiety reduction skills.	3. Introduce key coping strategies to be used as anxiety increases (including abdominal breathing, coping statements, and other diversion techniques).
4. Expose client to feared object or situation through imagery.	4. Develop and work though a hierarchy-based program of imagery desensitization.

5. Expose client to feared object or situation through *in vivo* desensitization.

5. Use the same or modified hierarchy to incrementally expose client to feared object or situation while using appropriate anxiety reduction skills.

Diagnosis: 300.29 Specific Phobia

Appendix 5

Visualization for Success

The following visualization can be used to help clients gain confidence about confronting and mastering a particular phobic situation. The visualization involves having the client fully see themselves in their phobic situation. It's best to work with it *after* having used imagery desensitization to overcome any anxiety that can come up initially when the client first visualizes dealing with their phobia. If this visualization causes anxiety, have the client go back and work up to it gradually using imagery desensitization.

Take a few moments to imagine what you'll be doing and how you'll feel when you have successfully reached the goal you've set for yourself. See yourself fully involved in what used to be your phobic situation . . . doing what you want to do . . . feeling calm, comfortable, and confident . . . (Allow about one minute to visualize yourself successfully handling a situation you've been avoiding.)

You know that there is no longer any need to avoid this situation. You can find yourself in this situation feeling calm, safe, and assured. As you enter this situation, your breathing is calm and regular and all of your muscles are fully relaxed. It's truly easy to enter this situation and it feels just fine. You experience a sensation of relaxation all over . . .

You've succeeded in reaching your goal, and you feel proud of yourself for having reached it. You're feeling confident that you can handle this situation every time you return to it. It feels great to have the freedom to enter this situation . . . to have fully achieved your goal . . . to have fully left the past behind . . . to be able to do what you want. Your life is enlarged by your success.

You can be calm and at ease whenever you're in this particular situation . . . in fact, it doesn't really matter a lot one way or the other. You find being in this situation to be just routine . . . nothing special . . . just a part of everyday life. Comfortable . . . easy . . . calm . . . just fine. And you're happy to know that you've succeeded . . . you've reached your goal . . . gained the mastery of yourself that you've wanted all along. You can enjoy life fully now . . . knowing that you feel safe and confident whenever you enter this particular situation. You truly enjoy your success and the freedom of choice you've gained.

Now take a few minutes once again to imagine how you would *think, act, and feel,* having achieved your goal with this particular situation . . . See yourself handling the situation in just the way you would like. . ..

Notice what you're doing . . . (15 seconds or more)

Notice how you appear . . . perhaps you see a smile of confidence on your face . . . How does your face express your success and your sense of accomplishment? (15 seconds or more)

Now notice the inner feeling of accomplishment you feel deep inside . . . Can you feel that wonderful feeling of satisfaction you've gained from your success? (15 seconds or more)

Perhaps you might also notice friends and family in the picture, and the good feelings they express about your success. Can you see them expressing their good feelings toward you now? (15 seconds or more)

Now that you know you've reached your goal, take a little time to imagine how you would enjoy the new freedom you've gained in your life. Are there any new opportunities available to you now that you have more freedom? You might see yourself enjoying these opportunities now. (Allow up to 1 minute.)

References

American Psychiatric Association. 1994. *Diagnostic and Statistical Manual of Mental Disorders—Fourth Edition (DSM-IV)*, Washington, D.C.: American Psychiatric Association.

Agras, Stewart. 1985. *Panic: Facing Fears, Phobias and Anxiety*. New York: W. H. Freeman.

Barlow, David. 1988. *Anxiety and Its Disorders*. New York: Guilford Press.

———. 1993. *Clinical Handbook of Psychological Disorders*. New York: Guilford Press.

Beck, Aaron T. 1979. *Cognitive Therapy and the Emotional Disorders*. New York: Meridian.

Beck, Aaron T., and Gary Emery. 1981. *Anxiety Disorders and Phobias: A Cognitive Perspective*. New York: Basic Books.

Bourne, Edmund. 1995. *The Anxiety and Phobia Workbook*, 2nd ed. Oakland: New Harbinger Publications.

Bourne, Edmund. 1992. "The Agoraphobia Treatment Group." In *Focal Group Psychotherapy*. Matthew McKay and Kim Paleg. Oakland: New Harbinger Publications.

Brown, Duane. 1996. *Flying Without Fear*. Oakland: New Harbinger Publications.

Chambless, D. L. 1989. "Spacing of Exposure Sessions in the Treatment of Phobia." Poster presented at the twenty-third Annual Convention of the Association for the Advancement of Behavior Therapy. New York.

Craske, M. and D. Barlow. 1993. "Panic Disorder and Agoraphobia". In *Clinical Handbook of Psychology Disorders.* 2nd ed., edited by D. Barlow. New York: Guilford Press.

Emmelkampf, P. M. G., and A. C. M. Kuipers. 1979. "Agoraphobia: Follow-up Study Four Years After Treatment." *British Journal of Psychiatry* 128:86–89.

Emmelkamp, P. 1982. *Phobic and Obsessive-Compulsive Disorders: Theory, Research, and Practice.* New York: Plenum Press.

Foa, E. B., J. S. Jameson, R. M. Turner, and L. L. Payne. 1980. "Massed vs. Spaced Exposure Sessions in the Treatment of Agoraphobia." *Behaviour Research and Therapy,* 18:333–338.

Garssen, B., C. deRuiter, and R. van Dyck. 1992. "Breathing/Retraining: A Rational Placebo?" *Clinical Psychology Review.* 12:141–153.

Hadley, Josie. 1996. *Hypnosis for Change: A Manual of Proven Techniques,* 3rd ed. Oakland: New Harbinger Publications.

Hardy, Arthur, B. 1986. *TERRAP Program Manual.* Menlo Park, Calif.: TSC Publications.

Jacobson, Edmund. 1974. *Progressive Muscle Relaxation.* Midway Reprint. Chicago: University of Chicago Press.

Jansson, L., and L. Ost. 1982. "Behavioral Treatments for Agoraphobics: An Evaluative Review." *Clinical Psychology Review* 2:311–336.

Jansson, L., A. Jerramalm, and L. G. Ost. 1986. "Follow-up of Agoraphobic Patients Treated with Exposure In-vivo or Applied Relaxation." *British Journal of Psychiatry* 149:486–490.

Lucas, Winafred B., ed. 1993. *Regression Therapy: A Handbook for Professionals.* Vol. I. Crest Park, CA: Deep Forest Press.

Marks, I. M., and A. M. Mathews. 1978. "Brief Standard Self-rating for Phobic Patients." *Behavior Research and Therapy* 17:236–267.

Mathews, A. M., M. G. Gelder, and D. W. Johnston. 1981. *Agoraphobia: Nature and Treatment.* New York: Guilford Press.

Mavissakalian, M., and D. H. Barlow. 1981. *Phobia: Psychological and Pharmacological Treatment.* New York: Guilford Press.

Meichenbaum, Donald. 1974. "Self-Instructional Methods." In *Helping People Change,* edited by F. K. Kanfur and A. P. Goldstein. New York: Pergamon Press.

Munby, J., and D. W. Johnston. 1980. "Agoraphobia: The Long-term Follow-up of Behavioral Treatment." *British Journal of Psychiatry.* 137:418–427.

Rachman, S. J., M. G. Craske, K. Tallman, and C. Solyom. 1986. "Does Escape Behavior Strengthen Agoraphobic Avoidance?" A replication. *Behavior Therapy.* 17:366–384.

Ross, Jerilyn. 1994. *Triumph Over Fear.* New York: Bantam Books.

Rothbaum, Barbara. 1997. "Virtual Reality Treatment for Phobias." Paper presented at seventeenth annual conference of The Anxiety Disorders Association of America. New Orleans.

Shapiro, Francine. 1995. *Eye Movement Desensitization and Reprocessing: Basic Principles, Protocols, and Procedures*. New York: Guilford Press.

Weeks, Claire. 1978. *Hope and Help for Your Nerves*. New York: Bantam Books.

———. 1978. *Peace from Nervous Suffering*. New York: Bantam Books.

Wolpe, Joseph and David Wolpe. 1988. *Life Without Fear*. Oakland: New Harbinger Publications.

Zeurcher-White, Elke. 1995. *An End to Panic*. Oakland: New Harbinger Publications.

Edmund Bourne, Ph.D., has specialized in treating anxiety disorders and related problems for almost two decades. He is author of the highly regarded *Anxiety & Phobia Workbook*, which has helped numerous people in the United States and other countries. For many years, Dr. Bourne was director of The Anxiety Treatment Center in San Jose and Santa Rosa, California. Currently he resides in Kona, Hawaii and in California.

Some Other New Harbinger Self-Help Titles

Dr. Carl Robinson's Basic Baby Care, $10.95
Better Boundries: Owning and Treasuring Your Life, $13.95
Goodbye Good Girl, $12.95
Being, Belonging, Doing, $10.95
Thoughts & Feelings, Second Edition, $18.95
Depression: How It Happens, How It's Healed, $14.95
Trust After Trauma, $13.95
The Chemotherapy & Radiation Survival Guide, Second Edition, $13.95
Heart Therapy, $13.95
Surviving Childhood Cancer, $12.95
The Headache & Neck Pain Workbook, $14.95
Perimenopause, $13.95
The Self-Forgiveness Handbook, $12.95
A Woman's Guide to Overcoming Sexual Fear and Pain, $14.95
Mind Over Malignancy, $12.95
Treating Panic Disorder and Agoraphobia, $44.95
Scarred Soul, $13.95
The Angry Heart, $13.95
Don't Take It Personally, $12.95
Becoming a Wise Parent For Your Grown Child, $12.95
Clear Your Past, Change Your Future, $12.95
Preparing for Surgery, $17.95
Coming Out Everyday, $13.95
Ten Things Every Parent Needs to Know, $12.95
The Power of Two, $12.95
It's Not OK Anymore, $13.95
The Daily Relaxer, $12.95
The Body Image Workbook, $17.95
Living with ADD, $17.95
Taking the Anxiety Out of Taking Tests, $12.95
The Taking Charge of Menopause Workbook, $17.95
Living with Angina, $12.95
Five Weeks to Healing Stress: The Wellness Option, $17.95
Choosing to Live: How to Defeat Suicide Through Cognitive Therapy, $12.95
Why Children Misbehave and What to Do About It, $14.95
When Anger Hurts Your Kids, $12.95
The Addiction Workbook, $17.95
The Mother's Survival Guide to Recovery, $12.95
The Chronic Pain Control Workbook, Second Edition, $17.95
Fibromyalgia & Chronic Myofascial Pain Syndrome, $19.95
Flying Without Fear, $12.95
Kid Cooperation: How to Stop Yelling, Nagging & Pleading and Get Kids to Cooperate, $12.95
The Stop Smoking Workbook: Your Guide to Healthy Quitting, $17.95
Conquering Carpal Tunnel Syndrome and Other Repetitive Strain Injuries, $17.95
Wellness at Work: Building Resilience for Job Stress, $17.95
An End to Panic: Breakthrough Techniques for Overcoming Panic Disorder, Second Edition, $17.95
Living Without Procrastination: How to Stop Postponing Your Life, $12.95
Goodbye Mother, Hello Woman: Reweaving the Daughter Mother Relationship, $14.95
Letting Go of Anger: The 10 Most Common Anger Styles and What to Do About Them, $12.95
Messages: The Communication Skills Workbook, Second Edition, $13.95
Coping With Chronic Fatigue Syndrome: Nine Things You Can Do, $12.95
The Anxiety & Phobia Workbook, Second Edition, $17.95
The Relaxation & Stress Reduction Workbook, Fourth Edition, $17.95
Living Without Depression & Manic Depression: A Workbook for Maintaining Mood Stability, $17.95
Coping With Schizophrenia: A Guide For Families, $13.95
Visualization for Change, Second Edition, $13.95
Postpartum Survival Guide, $13.95
Angry All the Time: An Emergency Guide to Anger Control, $12.95
Couple Skills: Making Your Relationship Work, $13.95
Self-Esteem, Second Edition, $13.95
I Can't Get Over It, A Handbook for Trauma Survivors, Second Edition, $15.95
Dying of Embarrassment: Help for Social Anxiety and Social Phobia, $12.95
The Depression Workbook: Living With Depression and Manic Depression, $17.95
Men & Grief: A Guide for Men Surviving the Death of a Loved One, $13.95
When the Bough Breaks: A Helping Guide for Parents of Sexually Abused Children, $11.95
When Once Is Not Enough: Help for Obsessive Compulsives, $13.95
The Three Minute Meditator, Third Edition, $12.95
Beyond Grief: A Guide for Recovering from the Death of a Loved One, $13.95
Hypnosis for Change: A Manual of Proven Techniques, Third Edition, $13.95
When Anger Hurts, $13.95

Call **toll free, 1-800-748-6273,** to order. Have your Visa or Mastercard number ready. Or send a check for the titles you want to New Harbinger Publications, Inc., 5674 Shattuck Ave., Oakland, CA 94609. Include $3.80 for the first book and 75¢ for each additional book, to cover shipping and handling. (California residents please include appropriate sales tax.) Allow two to five weeks for delivery.

Prices subject to change without notice.